With a Cherry on Top:

Stories, Poems, Recipes & Fun Facts from Michigan Cherry Country

With a Cherry on Top:

Stories, Poems, Recipes & Fun Facts from Michigan Cherry Country

by Angela Williams

Edited by Judith Kerman

MAYAPPLE PRESS 2006

Published by MAYAPPLE PRESS
408 N. Lincoln St.
Bay City, MI 48708
www.mayapplepress.com

ISBN 0-932412-41-6

Excerpt from *Pulling Down the Barn*, by Anne-Marie Oomen, pg. 87-90, reprinted with the permission of Wayne State University Press.

Excerpt from *Vamped, A Novel* by David Sosnowski, reprinted with the permission of The Free Press, A Division of Simon & Schuster Adult Publishing Group. Copyright © 2004 by David Sosnowski. All rights reserved.

"Cherry Pie" was previously published in the *Beloit Poetry Journal*, Spring 2004, and in *The Fingernail of Luck* (Mayapple Press, 2005).

"Sour Pie Cherries" was previously published in *bite to eat place* (Redwood Coast Press, 1995).

"The Edge" was previously published in *Quercus Review* (2004).

"In a Cherry Orchard" was previously published in *Tar River Poetry* 37:1

This book was designed and typeset by Judith Kerman in Adobe Caslon and Bell Gothic MT with Ancient Script titles: cover titles and text in Lucida Sans.

Cover photo courtesy of Cherry Marketing Institute; back cover photo courtesy of Jim Fredrickson. Photos not otherwise credited are by Angela Williams.

For Joe and Luanne, who made me one very starry night under the Leonid showers.—Angela

A Guide to Cherry Country

In the beginning 3
Recipe: Cherry Bounce 4
Story: Cherry Barge, *Meggan Carney-Ross* 6

In the orchards 13
Poem: In a Cherry Orchard..., *Jackie Bartley* 13
Recipe: Cherry Jam 20
Poem: Cherry Picking, *Robert McDonough* 22
Memoir: From "Picking cherries...," *Helen Westie* 24
Memoir: Water Jugs, *Anne-Marie Oomen* 26
Memoir: An Orchard Upbringing, *Emily Betz Tyra* 30
Poem: after the fire, *Alisa Gordaneer* 34
Essay: Farmer's Conversation, *Anne-Marie Oomen* 35
Recipe: Yogurt Smoothie 38
Recipe: Cherry Granola 38
Poem: Honeymoon, Torch Lake,
          Rebecca Emlinger Roberts 39

Celebration time 41
Poem: ACHOO!, *Evalyn Torrant* 42
Poem: Wallace Stevens, Mr. Cherry; ...
          MaryAnn Samyn 43
Recipe: Lu's Cherry Fruit Crunch 46
Recipe: Ginger-Spiced Cherries—a relish 48

Getting to work 51
Article: Fields of Dreams, *Juan A. Marinez* 54
Poem: The Silence That Follows, *Gerry LaFemina* 61
Poem: After the Pack, *Norman Veliquette* 65

The pies have it 67
Poem: Cherry Pie, *Conrad Hilberry* 67
Poem: The Edge, *Rhoda Janzen* 70
Recipe: Mother Mac's Cherry Pie 71
Recipe: E.Z. Pie Crust 72
Poem: Sour Pie Cherries, *Barbara Crooker* 73
Recipe: Classic Cherry Pie 74
Poem: Cherry Pantoum, *Pamela Ditchoff* 75

On top 77
Poem: Packing Cherry Cordials, *Judith Kerman* 79
Recipe: Chocolate Cherry Bombs 81
Poem: Engagement, *Judith Kerman* 82
Essay: From "The Poetics of Cherry," *Anita Skeen* 83

Fresh faces and phases 89
Recipe: Cherry Bread Pudding 93
Recipe: Michelle's Cherry Margarita 102
Recipe: Cherry Chocolate Martini 102
Recipe: Johnnie's Cherry Bomb 103
Poem: Sugar Freeze, *Bruce White* 103

Everything but the squeal 107
Poem: The Pits, *Adrienne Lewis* 107
Poem: garnets, *Alisa Gordaneer* 110
Novel Excerpt: Vamped, *David Sosnowski* 115
Poem: Climbing Cherry Trees, *Linda Nemec Foster* 119

Acknowledgements 120
Information & Resources 121
Contributors 122

In the beginning. . .

Photo courtesy of Jim Fredrickson

If there had been no lumbering era in Northern Michigan, there would be no cherry industry. Not only did Michigan's forests play a major role in the development of the state, but in agriculture as well.

The highly acidic sandy soil left by the glaciers grew tremendous pine forests. Shortly after Michigan became a state, a significant amount of its 750,000 acres of land was promised to members of the St. Mary's Falls and Ship Canal Company as payment for building the Soo Locks in Sault Ste. Marie. Many of the Company's members became lumber barons or chose to sell their holdings to logging developers. Prices rose as land changed hands and the lumbering era boomed. Between 1860 and 1890 the state produced more than 200 billion board feet of lumber from 1 billion trees.

Unfortunately, in their hasty production of lumber, not many logging entrepreneurs considered the effects of their companies' efforts on the land. There were few if any attempts at reforestation. The land was stripped and prone to fires. The acidic nature of the soil itself made it virtually useless for most farming, but the logging companies still profited by selling it to naïve settlers as fertile farmland. A great number of those farmers quickly went bankrupt, and the State of Michigan reclaimed the abandoned farms, many of which are still held by the state today.

As the lumbering boom quieted and agriculture became dominant in the region, cherries became a staple crop in Northern Michigan.

Perhaps some of the hardworking, hard-drinking lumbermen chose to enjoy the unique pleasure of this treat:

4

Cherry Bounce:

Wash and stem cherries. Use only fruit that is without blemishes or soft spots. Fill a quart jar with cherries.

Pour 2 cups of sugar over fruit. Fill jar with vodka; leave about a half inch of headroom. Cover tightly with jar lid and store in a cool dark place until about Thanksgiving or Christmas.

The liquor is delicious and the cherries are literally intoxicating.

Can be made in larger quantities (a gallon). Just increase the amounts. Leave a bit more headroom.

Recipe courtesy of Charlotte Allen.

Although traditional crops failed to grow in the stripped lumber fields, many coastal areas were well-suited for fruit farming. The climate and the soil were right for it. Lake-effect weather, created as westerly winds cross Lake Michigan, can delay premature growth and extend the growing season until fruit reaches maturity.

The first cherry orchard in Northwestern Lower Michigan was planted in 1852 in Omena by Presbyterian minister Peter Dougherty, who came to the area as an Indian missionary. The trees flourished. Others noticed his success, and more cherry orchards were planted. By the 1900's, the cherry orchards had begun to proliferate on the region's rolling hills of sandy soil. The lay of the land and its proximity to the 45th parallel help make the cherry the right crop for the region's agriculture. Think of it in comparison to the Bordeaux region of France, also sharing that latitude, where similar crops have been successful. Because of its natural assets, Leelanau County surpasses all areas of the U.S. today in its cherry production. An estimated 12,250 acres are host to 1.3 million trees.

In an *Atlantic Monthly* article in 1870, author H.W.S. Cleveland spoke of a tour he'd taken of the Grand Traverse region. Cleveland stated that "apples and cherries attain their highest degree of perfection in this favored land." This was the first published reference to cherry growing in the region.

Most initial cherry orchards were part of general farming. A farm would grow enough of a variety of crops to sustain the families working it. Specialized crops were not usually planted, as self-sufficiency was the prevalent model of farming. In addition, transportation, refrigeration, storage, and marketing evolved just as the farming itself did; in the early years, they were not ready for large-scale specialty crops.

Many people believe that the Morgan farm preceded all others in the region in growing cherries. However, the first commercial cherry orchard was planted by John Kroupa in 1893 on the Ridgewood Farm on Old Mission Peninsula owned by O.H. Ellis. He later became a leading authority on cherries among farmers in the Grand Traverse region.

Early cherry crops were shipped by steamers and barges to Chicago, Milwaukee, and other ports. This was made easier when the first cherry cannery, "Cherry Home," was built by Francis Haserot, who owned a considerable amount of orchard property that fronted Grand Traverse Bay. The factory had a dock and dormitories for its workers in 1916. Smaller steamers would bring cherries from other orchards around the bay to the cannery to be processed as well.

Several more canneries cropped up in the Traverse City area. One of the most conspicuous was the Morgan plant, which later became the Morgan-McCool plant. Recycling and reuse of equipment has always been common within the industry, and much of the canning equipment recently dismantled at Triple D. Orchards, Inc., was originally from that plant. There was also a plant called the F and M plant, which packed citrus fruit from Florida and cherries from Michigan. Cherry Growers, Inc., which still operates in Grawn, Michigan, had its first plant on Grand Traverse Bay just east of where the Holiday Inn is located today. The Traverse City Canning Company building still stands on Eighth Street, east of Cass Road, currently housing Thirlby Automotive.

The days of the cherry steamers and barges are long gone but this piece by Meggan Carney-Ross easily takes us to that time and place.

Cherry Barge

Lou Ella's arms and back relaxed as she dropped her bag on the polished wood floor, crossed the kitchen, and with her tough little arms, hugged her round friend disguised in a full white apron and kerchief covering her red hair. Anne Marie and Lou Ella had known each other even before they had started at the Old Mission School walking part of the way together daily when the Masons lived at the Lamoreau farm. They had been in the Camp Fire Girls together. And when Anne Marie's mother died, she and her two brothers stayed with the Masons for awhile until Anne Marie moved in with a great aunt and the boys went with other relatives. They shared smokes, talked boys, walked back to the pioneer cemetery deep in the woods and plunged off the end of Haserot Pier cradling large rocks sinking themselves all the way to the sandy bottom of East Bay.

"So you didn't stow away after all?" Anne Marie asked. Lou Ella remembered the barge trip that Anne Marie was teasing her about. One summer day a few years ago Anne Marie and some of the other girls had gotten permission to ride a cherry barge from Haserot Pier on the east side of the peninsula around the end to Northport on the tip of the Leelanau peninsula to go to a dance and stay the night with someone's cousin. Lou Ella's mother refused to let her go because she was, "only fourteen and didn't need to be dancing with boys way over in Northport." But Lou Ella didn't listen; she was convinced that her mother was too hard on her. Her mother was afraid that she already paid too much attention to boys or that in the last few months they were paying a lot more attention to her anyway. Her mother saw the way the boys' bodies open toward her as she walks down the narrow aisles in the grocery store, the way their heads turn in windows of passing cars, the way groups engulf her on the sidewalks or in parking lots after a ball game or church service or school day.

Lou Ella had blossomed at thirteen. She had soft, wavy, brown hair. She was still small, but she had curves in the right places and a lovely face with an intoxicating smile. Regardless of her 5'2 height, she seemed taller because, always moving, she commanded attention and flirted with a quick wit and wry smile. She was smart, got good marks in school, but she was also in trouble frequently because she knew how smart she was and how much that didn't much matter for a farm girl in northern Michigan. She spent hours and hours sitting at a desk with other student troublemakers like toughie Bobby White, cut-up Gary Henderson and mean Martha Hernandez, who weren't allowed to talk, write or read. Just sit there staring at the walls, the desk, the floor and each other—the floor was made up of 358 shellacked vertical pine boards, only two more than the number of days in a year she had thought. Why was it a crime to crack your gum when someone was talking to you? Everybody cracks their gum. And why was it so bad to smoke in between classes? Some of the teachers even did. Or why was it wrong to point out to Doris Adams that the hair on her arms made her look like a monkey? It was the truth. Or why was it a crime to ask Mr. Denby, the Science teacher, why it always smelled like dead animals in the lab while sitting right next to those pickled eels, dead baby Opossums and long-legged frogs? It did. And she didn't want to have to smell dead things or what they were pickled in, not after Will, not after all the boys except the young and defective ones left, not after most of her friends quit school to work because of all the open jobs. And Lou Ella stayed in school to please her mother after she had pleaded with Lou Ella to finish school because she had not.

So she snuck on the barge after her mother had said no. A crystal clear summer day, it was one of those calm, perfect days dreamt about when the snow drifts up to the rooflines in January. The light green waters bled turquoise near the shore and darker blue as she walked out to the end of the pier where the barge waited packed with crates of cherries loaded by a modified tractor with forklift. The pier spread so wide that a forklift or a truck could turn all the way around on it and make a small girl feel on land even though she was suspended over water. Yet Lou Ella felt comfortable there knowing she could hold her breath longer than any one else she knew under that very same water. For that title, hadn't she beaten out Anne Marie's brother Marcus just last July? He came up sputtering and she smiling. . . she knew holding her breath was not just about having big lungs but about patience and the ability to contain panic and submerge it. For a moment she sees herself in the surface of the lake with a big rock cupped in her hands, arms sling-like. Her reflection is broken by the light breeze rippling the surface of the water, but below she is confident it is calm. So she jumps off, like she had hundreds of times. The water hits her toes, legs, bottom, torso, breast, neck, head in a rushing chill and then submersion. Plunging through the surface of the water so quickly that the small panic felt when moving from one world to another became only exhilaration and eventually just relief to be under the water in the quiet, the softness encases her.

But today she wasn't swimming. She had her best dress on, and she had arrived early in the morning before the other girls, before Mr. Dougan, the barge operator, so she could hide between the big wet crates of bulging, red shiny cherries. The fruit smelled like the salty and vinegary brine they'd been soaking in. The pickled, bloated frogs in glass cases of the science room and then the large dark pools of floating cherries outside the processing plants flashed in her mind. They were both suspended in something to stop decay, to halt what was only natural. A feeling like a shadow of loneliness and necessity fell on Lou Ella even though she and the dock were illuminated by the intense summer sun.

She found a spot near the back of the barge between the tanks and waited for hours until the girls arrived and punctual Mr. Dougan started the boat north up around the tip. She could hear the girls and Anne Marie talk about who was going to be there at the dance. That mean Miller boy who had called Anne Marie a cow, behind her back but loud enough for her to hear, had better not be there or she'd "sock him in the eye." And Al Munro, with his summer bleached brown hair and green eyes, was "the fella" they'd all hoped would be there. And Lou Ella didn't know who to hope would be there; she just wanted to be. And when Mr. Dougan stretched out his pudgy arm and pointed a wide finger toward the Old Mission Lighthouse to show the girls how far they were off shore, Lou Ella blew her chances. She had to pop her head up to see the lighthouse and maybe get a glimpse of Grandpa Tinker's farm which was someone else's now. Maybe she'd make out the cows on the shore as she and Will had followed them in the mornings and evenings to watch them drink, and she'd see her dog Shep waiting to bring them back. Or maybe she'd even catch sight of herself, a little girl, sitting by the water as she had nearly everyday recording all the changes of the sand and water and time. And maybe, just maybe, she'd set her eyes on. . . Will. Could that be where he really was, instead of on some boat in the Pacific? Bobbing like an oxygen-laden piece of fruit in a pool, maybe she was forced up, because she really just couldn't stand the caustic smell of brined cherries, suffocating her, her eyes tearing as she hid.

"Lou Ella Mason! What are you doing there!?" Mr. Dougan grumbled.

All the girls' faces swung around like the folds of a twirling skirt to see the top of Lou Ella's head pop back down between the crates. They all began to giggle with hands to their mouths while Anne Marie wiggled herself back between the crates to retrieve her.

"Lou Ella, what are you doing? You are in so much trouble with your Ma," Anne Marie said.

Lou Ella gave in by rising up and laughing, her eyes watering and red. Anne Marie couldn't help but laugh too.

"I told you I was gonna come anyways," Lou Ella said.

 Meggan Carney-Ross

10

If there had been no lumbering era in the region, there would be no cherry industry. And without bees, there would be no cherries. It's interesting to note that the region's cherry crops were dependent upon pollination by wild honeybees until the 1940's. It was then that growers began to build hives to breed their own bees. Keeping their hives was essential to crop success.

Photo courtesy of Neva Veliquette

Today, Cherry Bee, Inc., an affiliate of Cherry Ke, Inc., and Shoreline Fruit, Inc., runs 4000 to 6000 colonies. In order to keep their beehives active year-round, they lease their colonies to citrus growers in Florida, almond growers in California, and cranberry growers in Wisconsin. The bees then pollinate star thistle in August before the fall harvest of honey. Cherry Bee, Inc., markets their honey as well as pollination services. Over a five month period each year, these bees sample a unique variety of crops, making for a special blended flavor.

11

Pollination is crucial to the industry. Cherry varieties that have been around for quite a while are relatively easy to pollinate, although other elements present challenges for those types of trees. But the newer varieties such as Balatons, a sweet-tart cherry developed by horticulturists from Michigan State University, are currently creating difficulties for growers because the traditional methods of pollination are not working. Honeybees just aren't as attracted to the new varieties of trees. Recent experiments with importing different bees have had marginal success. There may be something in the nectar or pollen that repels the honeybees. Research also suggests that the Balatons may have a shorter period in which they are open for pollination. Cross-pollination of sweet cherries with Balatons may be part of the answer. With more research and experimentation, growers hope to be able to establish this new variety in the orchard and then the marketplace.

Photo of beekeeper Brad Webster of Cherry Bee, Inc., courtesy of Neva Veliquette

In the orchards. . .

Photo courtesy of Jim Fredrickson

In a Cherry Orchard Thinking of Edward Hopper

Jackie Bartley

Though you can't see the lake
from here, this light
is lake light, pale
rice paper blue
beneath which the pointillist push
of green-pink-white
is silent and strong
as seedling peas germinating under cement
in a grade school experiment,
a fervor of blossoms

held up as if in offering
by the burnt red, bony grip
of row on vanishing row
of cherry limbs.
                    And at their knees,
a small inland sea of dandelions
gone to seed, delicate as fossil rain.
Amid the drowsy hum of bee, the calls
of killdeer and meadowlark,
dozens of them wait to be shaken free,
dispersed by the patient breeze
that moves through this orchard
like a comb
drawn through a woman's dark hair,
a woman standing by a window
who pauses, perhaps,
to pull loose strands
from the comb
and, finding one white as chalk dust,
holds it up to the light,
her thoughts already traveling
to that place far out over water.

Early May brings the petals of cherry blossoms in Northern Michigan, weather permitting. And that means that in six weeks it will be time to begin the harvest. Cherry processors, growers, and others within the industry are scrambling to prepare for this critical time throughout the fallow period of winter and early spring months: readying equipment, observing and tending the orchards, recruiting workers, and projecting what will come of it all financially, personally, and somehow spiritually.

One of my favorite quotes comes from the movie *A League of Their Own*. Jimmy Dugan is conversing with Dottie Hinson about her leaving the team before the World Series. He says to her, "It's supposed to be hard. If it wasn't hard everyone would do it. The hard . . . is what makes it great." It's easy to understand this idea in the context of the cherry industry. Whether it's the farmers, their crews, or others involved, the adrenaline rush of the sports world can be felt during harvest time. But that rush first begins to tingle at the onset of cherry blossoms in May.

I don't want to imply a romanticized version of the farming life, as is done often enough in art, literature, and film. But it is rewarding, noble, and respectable to bring in a good crop and to do it well. In order to do so, many long hours are clocked by those directly involved in cherry production. Though the layman assumes that the old saying about blood, sweat, and tears applies in every season, they don't know the half of it.

Many aspects of the industry become a family affair, not necessarily by choice, but out of necessity. Running a family and business requires long hours of hard labor spent together. Whether it involves administrative work, the production line, trucking, apiaries, or work in the orchards, many Northern Michigan cherry farms and production plants are operated by families that have long histories in the business. Because of those long histories, advances can be made in the design of equipment for in-orchard use and for processing lines, better crop management can take place, new fruit varieties are developed, and more cherry products can then be made available for the general consumer.

A rewarding life in cherry farming can come from something as simple as knowing how to look at a tree because you've been in the orchards since you were a small child. Such is the case with Warren Deering, a cherry and apple farmer in Leelanau County. 15 He is 89 years old and still active in his farming. In fact, I have his orchards in view from my office window daily. I realize my good fortune in that respect, especially when the blossoms are peaking. There are few better sights than the trees in their thick, white, nearly rococo finery, anchored by grape hyacinths in each row.

In early July of 2004, Norm Wheeler, a teacher at the Leelanau School and editor of the *Glen Arbor Sun*, stopped in during harvest time to ask me, "Are you shakin' yet?" To which I replied, "No, not really. Haven't had that much coffee yet today. Only six cups, I think." He looked at me oddly, and I realized he meant the orchards across the street belonging to Warren. Were they shaking the trees yet? I clarified things and directed him to speak with Mr. Deering at the farm about the harvest. The result of Norm's interview with Warren was published in the *Glen Arbor Sun* in July of 2004:

When it comes to cherries, Warren Deering of Empire has seen it all. It's a sunny July morning, and Warren, almost 88 years old, is still out in the orchard. We watch the two halves of the shaker (driven by a man on each, Tom Lackey and Jeremy Knapp) cruise down the row and stop for about thirty seconds at each tree to shake its trunk. The leaves blur in the intense vibration, cherries drop in the gravity storm, bounce down the angled tarps to the conveyor belt, and ride up the elevator at one end of the shaker to spout into a tank of cold water. There's even a stream of air blowing through the falling curve of shiny red fruit to blow the leaves away.

Two tractor drivers (Frank Majszak and Charlie Baker) shuttle back and forth to the cooling pad with full tanks of cherries or fresh tanks of cold water supplied by Jonathan "Tim" Baatz, the fork lift operator and cooling pad master. Under Warren's supervision this neat and efficient operation requires only 5 men. But it wasn't always so simple. "I used to have 100 Mexican pickers living out here in tents," Warren reminisces. "We'd keep a tank of fresh water out for their drinking and cooking water." It was like that through the nineteen-fifties. Migrant workers from Mexico and south Texas flooded into West Michigan in big stake trucks. Tent villages sprouted up next to the big white clapboard farmhouse in the rows of fruit trees. Whole families, from the infants through the grandparents, picked the fruit in a feverish harvest through July and into August. If it was a wet summer the fruit could get brown rot. If a sudden thunderstorm blew through there could be hail damage or the cherries could be wind-whipped and the price would plummet. The livelihood of the local farmers and their communities, as well as that of the migrants, depended on a good year. From Shelby, Mears, and Hart in Oceana County, to Empire, East Leland, and Northport in Leelanau County, and on up

Old Mission Peninsula in Grand Traverse County, the local population of farm owners and the migrant population of Mexican farm workers toiled together in pretty much equal numbers every summer to get the fruit in.

Warren Deering reminded me of the farm workers' movement in the sixties that resulted in the many cinder block pickers' shacks being built, with toilets and showers replacing the outhouses, water spigots, and tanks of water that such huge numbers of migrants had been sharing in their tent villages for generations. I remember what Warren speaks about. I grew up in Shelby and picked both sweet and tart (then we called them "sour") cherries for 50 cents a lug, up and down the ladder on those hot, dusty, sticky summer days. My brother got to drive around on the tractor and hoist the lugs onto the trailer, marking down the chits on a clipboard as I and the Mexican boys I grew up with (Juan and Amadeo Reyna) and their families moved up and down the rows.

Suddenly in the mid nineteen-sixties, the Friday Tractor Company of Hartford, Michigan changed everything. They invented a hydraulic boom that mounted on a tractor, operated off its PTO, and could shake the cherries off the trees! No more hand-picking! It was amazing and revolutionary. My brother and I were on the crew of teenagers lining up boxes under the trees, then propping heavy half-moon shaped aluminum and nylon tarps on those boxes on either side of the tree. The tractor and boom pulled up, the driver jumped off and extended the boom into the cherry branches to clamp onto the bigger limbs, and the tree was rattled until all of the cherries and many of the leaves fell off. Limbs broke, the skin of the limbs got peeled off if the hydraulic grip was either too tight or too loose. We had another line of boxes waiting at the next tree and were ready to move the tarps and hoist the big boxes of heavy fruit upside down over the tanks of water, all at a dead run. We were a sticky and dirty and buff crew of sixteen-year-olds, and by the end of the harvest the white boys and the Mexican boys were all the same color. We were all one.

But in the sixties the more flexible hybrid trees that are grown to be shaken had yet to be developed by the horticulturalists at MSU. And the shaker itself was still an inexact mechanical process in its infancy. Warren Deering's super-efficient shaker of today resembles the old Fridays of 1967 only in purpose. "I had a Friday boom," Warren said, "and then a roll-up, and then a one-man shaker from Friday where the tarp wrapped around the tree and one man could run it. I sold it to Joe Shimek." By then Warren and his brothers Richard (who has passed away) and Mark (who still goes to work at Deering's Market in Empire most days though he's also in his eighties) had established Triple D. Orchards on Stormer Road. They built a fruit packing plant that produced, among other products, Glen Lake Apple Juice. A few years ago T.J. Keyes took over as owner and manager of the processing plant. Warren Deering still owns, grows, and harvests the fruit on the orchard side of Triple D. Orchards but uses the name Maple Valley Farms now.

"The way the commodities market works makes fruit-growing a tough business proposition," Warren explains, "Growers don't know what per pound price they'll get until after the harvest, when the processors know how much they've got to sell, and the marketing experts and the brokers in the industry know how much they can sell on the world-wide market, and for what price. So you grow the fruit, you watch the weather, and you hope."

Warren says, "Coloma Fruit is paying 40 cents cash per pound, same as last year. I'm selling my cherries to T.J. But what price we'll get? Nobody knows anything yet. It's the damnedest business you ever heard of," Warren chuckles, with a twinkle in his eye. "When they get through we'll get our 'share'! There's no use in hollering." And what about still working in the orchard at 87 years of age? "Oh, it's the best thing for me," Warren Deering assures. "You gotta have something to live for!"

Norm Wheeler

In the orchards, equipment development ripens to fruition. By the late 1960's the cherry shaker had revolutionized the cherry industry. Hand-picking has long gone by the wayside as it takes about 10 times as many man hours to pull a ton of cherries as it does to harvest a ton of other fruit. Using a shaker, 4-5 workers replace 250 needed to harvest the same amount of cherries. Harvesting costs within the industry with this development are reduced by about 50%.

A cherry shaker in operation.
Photos courtesy of Cherry Marketing Institute.

A de-stemmer unit in opertion.

Another equipment advance developed within the region was the in-orchard de-stemmer unit, which separates the fruit from the stem as it is harvested. This was developed by the Smeltzer brothers of Benzonia, Michigan in the 1960's. These are still in use, as well as the newer customized versions used on production lines at processing facilities. It is one more way to guarantee the quality of end-product cherries.

19

Technological innovation is a priority at Cherry Ke, Inc., a 1200-acre cherry orchard and processing operation in Kewadin, Michigan, near Elk Rapids. Owners Gene and Dean Veliquette and their brother Norman, plus other family members, were raised on a Northern Michigan dairy farm and have been involved in agriculture their entire lives. To survive in a no-growth market they concentrate on processing, marketing, and cost reduction. Gene's innovativeness in the orchard has led to developments in the design of wind machines for frost prevention, hedgers for tree trimming, and heavy-duty forklifts made from old pick-up trucks. One of his customized applicators applies fertilizer and herbicide at an acre per minute, four times faster than with conventional equipment.

The Veliquette matriarch, Marie Veliquette, is proud of her family's involvement and leadership in the industry. In addition, she makes some of the best jam, which she shares generously. Marie offers a tip for keeping the foam down on the boil: put in a little bit of butter while you stir.

Cherry Jam

1½ lbs. frozen unsweetened tart cherries
4 C granulated sugar
1 (1.75 oz.) powdered fruit pectin
¾ C water

Follow recipe exactly. Do not reduce or increase the amount of ingredients or substitute other ingredients. Do not double recipe because mixture may not set.

Have ready clean freezer containers with lids (1 or 2 cup size).

There are 4-5 cups of frozen cherries in 1½ pounds. Coarsely chop cherries while still frozen. Allow cherries to thaw and come to room temperature. Do not drain cherries; use all the juice for the jam. You should have 2 cups of chopped cherries and juice. It is critical that the cherries be at room temperature, not slightly chilled.

Combine chopped (room temperature) cherries with juice and sugar in medium mixing bowl; mix well. Set aside 10 minutes; stir occasionally.

Combine powdered fruit pectin and water in a small saucepan; mix well. (Mixture may be slightly lumpy before cooking.) Bring mixture to a boil over high heat, stirring constantly. Boil while stirring for 1 minute. Remove from heat. Immediately stir pectin mixture into cherries. Stir constantly until sugar is completely dissolved and no longer grainy, about 3 minutes. Quickly pour into containers to within ½ inch of tops. Wipe off top edges of containers; cover with lids. Let stand at room temperature 24 hours to set.

For immediate use, store in refrigerator up to 3 weeks, or freeze containers up to 1 year. To use, thaw in refrigerator.

This recipe makes 5 to 6 cups.

Recipe courtesy of Cherry Marketing Institute

"Cherry picking" can mean many things, and not always what we imagine.

Cherry Picking

Robert McDonough

I can't help thinking of my father.
The doctors called it cherry-picking, cutting
tumors out of his scalp, one by one
as they came, until there wasn't enough skin left
to stretch over the wounds.

That was a metaphor. This
is cherry picking on a hot August day,
she up on the step ladder, a little wobbly
but probably thinking she'd make
a lighter fall of it, I holding the bucket
up to her and working on lower branches,
the dogs somewhere nearby, safe enough
on this untravelled road. The cherries
are elusive, like marbles on springs
as she says, a figure I am so taken with
I forget the deer flies for a while,
but we keep picking and half fill the bucket.

22

That's poetry for you. Tumors
aren't cherries, and cherries aren't marbles,
but meanwhile we can stand the deer flies
and now we can make a cherry pie.
These woods are posted, not hers, but the trees
grow wild and no one will mind.
We've left plenty for the birds.

We've come a long way since this, baby:

23

Photo, c. 1910, courtesy of Benzie Area Historical Society

Empire resident Helen Westie wrote a piece on her childhood memories of picking cherries with her family during the 1930's. It appeared in the *Glen Arbor Sun's* August 12, 2004 issue.

From "Picking cherries during the Great Depression"

In the midst of the Great Depression, American families harvested the cherry crops here in Northern Michigan. They were the forerunners of the migrants who came much later.

It was 1931 and I was 13 years old when my family camped in the orchard of huge cherry trees at the tip of Old Mission Peninsula, which at that time consisted solely of cherry farms.

Our method of hand picking was a far cry from the cherry shaking described by Norm Wheeler in the July 29 issue of the *Glen Arbor Sun*. A pail was hooked onto our wide belts, leaving both hands free to scoop all the cherries from a branch into our pails. And we had to get them all. I wore my brothers' overalls or slacks because girls wore only dresses then. Blue jeans would not come into wide use until several decades later.

24

We started at the top of the tree and when a pail was full, we would climb down from the high ladder and empty it into a cherry lug—I was a good, enthusiastic picker and could earn almost a dollar a day. My father's daily wage was $1.50 or a little more. My two brothers, a little younger than I, were not as productive or motivated. My mother stayed back at the tent airing our bedding and packing our lunches. When she delivered them, she would stay and pick for a while.

Right from the start, she became friendly with the farmer's wife—they made an arrangement that my mother would bake two casseroles or two pie pasties (having been raised in the Upper Peninsula, she was an excellent pasty maker), one for us and one for the farmer's family, and we would eat dinner at our camp table.

Often after the day's work, the farmer, Mr. Kilmurray, let us three kids ride on the truck loaded with full cherry lugs to the canning factory in Traverse City. For the records, the truck drove onto a scale and after unloading was weighed again. There was a story told to us about an incident one year before.... When the farmers brought their loads to the factory, the price for sour cherries had gone way down. The farmers, in protest, dumped their whole day's pickings into Grand Traverse Bay. The whole bay was red with cherries as far as the eye could see, and the story and photographs appeared in newspapers throughout the United States.

My brothers and I regarded the very first cherry-picking year as the most wonderful adventure of our young lives. We had left our home in Dearborn, Michigan in early spring of that year. My Uncle Ed, who had hunted in this area, assured my parents that living here was much cheaper and there was always fruit picking for a little extra income. My mother and father were feeling desperate; every insurance policy had been cashed. Their life savings was all gone. There had been no work for my father for two years and now it meant going on welfare.

After two years, we heard from friends back home that the factories were hiring again, so of course we had to move back. I shed bitter tears because I was smitten with a senior boy. We had a sad good-bye and what I chose to think was True Love's First Kiss.

Helen Westie

Photo, c.1890, courtesy of Benzie Area Historical Society

Working in the orchards is a memory for many baby-boomers and their predecessors. It was a way of life, and a way of making due. Many farm families have sold out to developers or to larger farms that lease their acreage for crops, but the families are who they are because of the hard work required during their youth. The success of the crop was and is a priority. The whole family was expected to participate, as we can see depicted in "Water Jugs," reprinted from Anne-Marie Oomen's *Pulling Down the Barn*.

26

Water Jugs

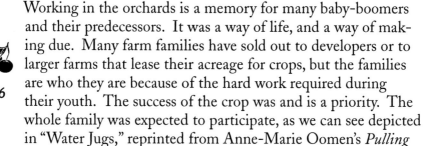

We pick cherries in the heat of July, at high summer. As I scramble in the trees, on the ladders, and on the ground where I have spilled the cherries, the dry blossoms fall and get caught in my collar and sleeves, and work down my back. They itch. The dust from the trucks flies up in my face, and the fruit makes my hands and arms sticky. If I wipe my sweat or scratch, the sticky gets wherever I put my hands, the itch gets worse. I learn not to put my hands anywhere I don't want to itch. The worst of it is being in a tree, which should be cool, because it's an orchard. But it's not. An orchard, planted densely and growing big healthy trees, stops a good summer breeze right on the perimeter. Inside an orchard, inside a tree, where the cherries are, where I am, it's hot.

The only real break happens when my mother asks one of us to go back to the house, to the well, to fill the water jugs. She uses this errand as a reward for hard work, and it usually goes to Rick, or even to Marijo, the littlest picker, because they are good, steady workers. I am not.

From the tree, I hear the voices of the Mendozas, the migrant family whom my father has hired this year. The trees have reached maturity, and the crop is now too large for our family to pick the ten acres alone. The Mendozas live in the old one-room schoolhouse, where a large shower and an indoor bathroom were recently installed. I am a little afraid of them. I do not yet identify them as individuals. Instead I apprehend them as a collective, a cluster of understated Spanish voices murmuring through the trees, like shy animals who belong here more than I do. They seem unaware of the heat, unaware of itching. They always wear long-sleeved shirts and long pants, and they rarely seem to sweat. Of the Mendoza family, I know only one by name, Miguel, a slim, dark-haired boy, exactly as tall as I am.

27

"Pick in your own tree," my mother tells me firmly, knowing my weakness for distraction, but I go to the tree where Miguel is picking or, if my mother is in the orchard, I go to the tree nearest the one his family is picking. Early in the morning I listen to the cherries drop into the empty buckets. The soft thud is a tiny percussion, a heartbeat coming and going in the heat. I think he looks at me sometimes through the laden branches.

I wait for Miguel to speak but he never does, though once I hear him answer his own mother briefly, softly, in Spanish. Another time, as I carry a bucket back to the lugs on the truck, I pass him as we shuffle through fescue and orchard grasses. He smiles and nods, a gesture laced with such politeness that his reserve forever becomes a gauge for something I eventually associate with manners but for which true courtesy is the better description. Shyly, I smile back.

That day the orchard fills with the sound of starlings, their glossy black song scrilling among the branches and down the rows, and the rich drumming as pails full of tart cherries pour into empty lugs on the tailgate of the old Chevy truck. Over the long days that follow, I come to care for Miguel's quiet. When I listen for him, what I hear are the unwords from the rest of the orchard. When I can't manage to pick near his tree, the itching is worse, my day hotter and more miserable. I climb a ladder and sit in the high branches, and I pick so slowly I fill barely a lug throughout the entire morning.

I am in the ladder, having picked across from Miguel's tree for most of the day. I have a pail full of cherries, and as I swing down the steps, moving in mid-air, the old canvas harness, worn from many summers, breaks at the buckle where the snap latches onto the handle of the pail. The cherries tumble down in a bright red waterfall into the sand and grasses. I climb down step-by-step, kneel at the bottom of the ladder, and begin picking them up with sticky fingers that quickly become caked with sand and mud. I am so tired I have forgotten to be embarrassed, forgotten to be ashamed. I do not even realize he is there until his dark hands dart into my vision, lifting the cherries quickly and dropping them back into the bucket. Our hands alternate, hovering over the bucket, dropping in the cherries. When we have collected as many as we can, I try to say the one word I think I remember from *I Love Lucy*: "Grachi-as."

His mother chuckles softly from a nearby tree. He calls something back to her. I wait, but he turns and moves back into the shadows of branches and fruit.

The next day I come back, this time wearing an old belt around my waist and it pulls against my back as the bucket gets heavier with cherries. At noon I unbuckle the belt and bucket, setting them down under the tree I will begin picking after lunch. I think no one can see, so I lift my shirt, twisting, and touch the raw welts that have begun to rise where the leather rubs against the top of my hips. I walk slowly to the truck where my mother, frowning, divides up bologna sandwiches, carrot sticks, and cake. We pass the water jug, beaded with icy water, from hand to hand, mouth to mouth.

When I return to the tree, the leather belt is gone. In its place a regular canvas shoulder harness rests across from the pail. I look around but there is no sound among the trees. Here and there, in the farther rows, I can see the lower torso of some picker or the back of someone's shirt, crossed by the dark harnesses, moving into the thick branches. No one is near, not anyone from my family, not anyone from the Mendozas. Not Miguel. But out of the quiet I hear the rise of the summer insects, the flies and the bees, the purpose and need in their hum. I say nothing. But all the rest of the day I pull the cherries off the branches as if there was nothing that mattered so much in the world. I pull them off with a fervor and meaning that must get attention.

Late in the afternoon my mother idles the truck through the trees, picking up stacked lugs—checking, always checking, to see that every tree is topped. She sees my loaded lugs under the tree. She looks at me quietly, pulls the empty water jugs from the floor of the truck and hands them to me, saying merely, "Be sure to rinse them out first."

It is magic.

With the plastic milk jugs swinging loose in my arms, I run through the long rows all the way to the house. I stand by the well-pit, where the air comes up from the pump cool as a cave, and breathe in the chill musk of the underground. Here the grass is lushly chilled and matted from the spilled water. I take my shoes off. I listen to the hollow, gurgling sound of the jugs filling. I rinse my face and hands, putting my mouth around the tube of water from the hose for a long time and letting it slosh against my tongue. I stay there until I feel guilty, until my sweat has dried and I have summer on my skin, not in the heat, but in the cool comfort and into the honor of the water jugs. I heft them up and into my new arms like babies I will carry back to the still orchards. When this is done, I walk slowly back through the rows and rows of regular trees, letting the gallon orbs slosh against my arms. I walk and walk until I find the one tree. There, as the chosen one, I offer up first to Miguel the cool plastic jug as though it were a goblet of fine wine.

Anne-Marie Oomen

We've all been told that hard work builds character. Another perspective on this is provided by Emily Betz Tyra, whose essay first appeared in *Traverse the Magazine* in August 2000.

 ## An Orchard Upbringing

30

I once was too cool to eat cherries. In college I scraped maraschino off my grapefruit half and hid it in the corner of my cafeteria tray. Fresh sweet cherries didn't tempt me. I ate all the LifeSavers but the red ones. It's not that I didn't think cherries tasted good, they did, it's just to me they had become boring. Ordinary. Growing up on a cherry farm in Omena, that plump little fruit was as everyday as milk with dinner. But now I find myself living a final summer in my family's stone farmhouse before finding an apartment of my own, I understand better my debt to the cherries and the branches that held them.

In the beginning, the orchard was a fourth playmate for my older brother, little sister, and me. My brother foraged the rows for animal tracks. My sister and I spent hours tearing past the outskirts of the orchard on training wheels, singing Anne Murray's "There's A Hippo In My Tub" in vibrato soprano. We all loved watching the fruit turn from runty and green to fleshy and deep red or purple.

But come harvest, our romping ground morphed into a muddy ravine. The growls of the tractors and shakers drowned out our tiny voices. We watched from the porch when the shaker's mighty arms clamped around the tree's trunk and shook it like a toy rattle. Strong boys pulled out the tarps to catch the harvested fruit. The earth quaked beneath us.

With these rites of harvest came rites of passage for us. The cherries taught us our first lesson in finance, what it meant to sweat for our pay. At 14, my brother joined those boys pulling tarps, waking at 5 a.m. each day to work the orchards. I think that first summer might have made him a man. He was ornery and filthy when he got home. His head was full of horrific allergies. It was full, too, of pride in his burly and newly acquired biceps. My mom pitched his work clothes at the end of the summer. "I'm sacrificing them to the cherry gods," she said.

My younger sister and I also sought out lucrative possibilities in the orchard. After a treacherous windstorm one year, we went to all the fallen, fruit-heavy boughs and gathered quarts of cherries to sell. We set up our picnic table on M-22 just south of Northport and made a killing selling them for a dollar each. My six-year-old sister was convinced that if we could sell tart cherries as well as the sweets she'd have enough in the end to buy a horse.

The orchard was my sanctuary too. Its thick trees and steep hills were the perfect camouflage for a runaway nine-year-old, Strawberry Shortcake suitcase in tow. I could watch the house without my parents seeing me, to see how long it took for them to miss me and begin crying to the cherry gods for my safe return.

When I turned 13, I joined the ranks of farm hands. My lesson that summer was in vanity, as in, It Cannot Exist When Elbow-deep in Crates of Black Sweet Cherries. The sun made my face a mess of freckles. The cherry juice stained my hands purple. I'd have been lavender-hued for months if my brother hadn't demonstrated an ancient cherry farmer's secret; to get rid of dark sweet cherry stains, crush a few tarts in your palms and let the acidic juices work their magic.

Farm work made me tough. Well, tougher, anyway. I stuck out 12-hour days in the rain and learned not to flinch when I saw a tree snake. I laughed with harvest crew guys when teased about my bright turquoise lunch cooler (they called it my "Queenie Pail"). At break time my brother and I would compare the lunches our mom packed. We'd laugh when we pulled out our ham sandwich and lovingly sealed Ziploc baggies full of fresh sweet cherries. "We're in the middle of an orchard," my brother would say. My mom called it eating like a farmer.

Yesterday I ate the cherry on my milkshake. I thought of all that fruit has meant to my life and couldn't help appreciating its sweetness. I owe so much to the orchard in my backyard. It played with me, fed me, taught me, and loved me. Its fruit is anything but ordinary.

32

Emily Betz Tyra

A view of an approaching storm in the orchards of Fredrickson Farms in Empire, Michigan. Photo courtesy of Jim Fredrickson.

There are many variables involved when people are dependent upon Mother Nature for an income. If the petals don't come in time, or if the frosts come hard, or if the pollination is affected by the cold, or if the winds are too strong, crops are affected. Fear, following the weather and the almanacs, and trying to do the best one can to prepare for harvest are inherent to the life of anyone involved in agriculture.

33

The summer of 2002 was the most recent time when the fears of people in the cherry industry were realized. Cherry crops failed in Northern Michigan. There had been early warmth, early budding, and then heavy frosts followed by rains and winds. There was no hope to salvage much of anything. The summer before had yielded one of the largest harvests known to the area, so there was product in reserve for consumers, but it was a lost summer to many in the cherry industry. There simply was no crop.

Desolation comes in many forms. Alissa Gordaneer shares another:

after the fire

Alisa Gordaneer

its charred roof beams
like a chicken carcass after dinner:
we return to see what is left between them, curious
about the woman who hung blue net
around her trees, who kept five tabby cats
curled around her legs, whom
they say was sleeping
when it happened.

her walls are ribbed, like windows breathing acrid air
open to June sky.
a curtain flutters itself, a flame of
charred lace.

in the yard, the blue mesh has fallen,
gathered garnets in its folds:
you lean into the smell of cherries mixed
with sulfur, with smoke, and reach, gather
an unclaimed bounty. she'd want us to
enjoy, want us to taste. maybe she's watching
from somewhere.

34

like you watched the firefighters from across the street,
their chemicals
powdering flames with a wash of pink.
it is all poisoned now, the yard, the house,
your memory of her giving you dimes for every bucket,
how you would spit stones at the cats, wait
on the porch for pie.

you look down into your skirt, billowed with cherries,
the pink powder rising even now, your bounty
red, all these tastes of something
you cannot eat.

Farmers do know a few ways to combat the terrorism of nature against an emerging crop. Anne-Marie Oomen touches upon one of them in this essay that appeared in *Traverse the Magazine.*

Farmer's Conversation

Weather obsesses farmers. The cycle of frost and thaw are so important that some farmers will not say hello before they ask, "How cold was it at your place last night?" My father was a man who showed friendliness by explaining the weather to you. "See that cloud line? Cold front coming." If my father talked with me about weather, he was saying he loved me. If he did this with men or my friends, he was showing respect.

It is a Friday night in May and I am a sophomore in high school and my friends are coming to play guitar and sing songs in our half remodeled garage. I help my mother dust barnwood sills, shake braided rugs. As I clean, I fantasize about taking a late walk with Nick, the boy I like, through our blooming moonlit orchard.

Then on the 6:00 local news—hard frost warnings. Even then, I don't think about the weather except to wonder if it will be too cold to kiss under the trees. I don't see my father watching the thermometer all evening. I don't see my mother pace the kitchen, looking out at the orchard where my dad drives the pick-up through the rows. I am too self-absorbed to see him walk out among the trees and will away the cold. I am having friends to my house. I am thinking about kisses.

They arrive. It is the sixties but we live in a community so rural that it will be two years before bell-bottom jeans and big collars hit our world. We talk about "hippies" as though they are aliens. The Viet Nam War is a vague threat too far away to worry about—though before we graduate college, two of the boys in that room will go. The summer of love hasn't been conceived of yet. We make pizza from a box. I pick out the chords to "Blowing in the Wind" on the guitar.

We stack Beatles forty-fives onto the spindle, push aside the second-hand chairs and dance to "Help, I need somebody. . ." The cold is something we slip into only to dry our sweat before the next song drops.

At eleven o'clock his dark shadow enters the house. I am barely aware of my parents in the kitchen, talking in a tone which, if I had been listening, I would have recognized as desperation laced with cold. But when my father comes into this room, his face is dark and he smells of diesel and I know. We turn quiet, looking at him. He looks back at Cliff, at Nick, at all of us, a mix of kids who have grown up in rural life so thick with weather trouble that we can sense it the way city kids can foretell rush hours and unsafe streets. It is there in my father's breathing. His words vary the Beatles song, "I need some help, somebody to. . ." It is all he needs to say. He hands them work gloves, my mother passes out old sweaters so school jackets won't get filthy. I hurriedly pull on jeans and sweat shirts, and two girl friends will help if we can find old clothes. My mother calls parents to inform them of this peculiar draft.

36

Out in that world of frail blossoms and cutting chill, we follow the pick-up through the trees. My father shoves bales of heavy hay off the tailgate. Someone carefully lights each bale, one or two under every few trees. Too compact and green to burn, the bales smolder and warm smoke rises, carrying with it the few degrees that may, if we are very lucky, prevent freezing. As I bend I wonder why he isn't using smudge pots, then remember his complaints about the price of oil. He doesn't have to pay for the hay. I listen to my siblings and friends move erratically among the trees. "Blowing in the Wind" runs in my head, and I know, if the wind would come up, this spotty warmth would circulate, but it is still as a stone between those rows. I sing crazily, "How many rows must a man walk down. . ." No one laughs. The moon rises so brightly it douses the stars of this bitterly beautiful night where I had hoped to kiss. I walk and bend and lift. There is only hard breathing, the groan of the pick-up on the slopes, the thunk of bales hitting the dirt, the dull lisp of torches—the hard chords of work permeating the ephemeral and silent grace of cherry blossoms, their sweetness stained with last fall's last cutting of alfalfa and clover.

We reach the high east hilltop of the orchard at one, the moon pouring shrill light down on this night landscape. From here, rising above the orchard, supported by coils of hay-fed smoke, we see the dark wreath. We can look down into the orchard where, through the thick air, the low flame of an ignited bale gleams to ash. The orchard is an island clotted with a gray snake, floating on black grass. My father, looking west, points to a line of low darkness, "Front moving in," he says softly. He looks at us. In the silver dark, he takes off his gloves, nods into our smeared faces, shakes hands. "Go to the house," he says. "There will be coffee."

We walk down into the orchard, barely able to see through the haze. Nick takes my dirty hand in his. We walk slowly all the way. We do not talk. We do not kiss. The blossoms darken with smudge and future.

Anne-Marie Oomen

37

When the weather is good and the crops come in as hoped, it is what some call "crunch" time. To bring in the many millions of pounds of cherries the industry is regularly known for, it takes many people working many hours around the clock. If you do it right you can make some good money during those weeks of harvest. Dave and Judy Amon worked the cherry harvest in Hart in the 1960's, when they were first married. Today they're still working in the industry together but in a much larger and much more responsible capacity, as owners of Amon Orchards Farm Market and Bakery in Acme, Michigan. The optimism of their youth in the industry has extended into the present, with the many cherry products their business offers, seasonal tours of their orchards during cherry and apple seasons, and their involvement with the National Cherry Festival.

An easy recipe to start the day with comes from the Amons.

Yogurt Smoothie

8 oz. vanilla yogurt
1 oz. cherry concentrate
1 banana
½ C frozen raspberries or other fruit
¼ C frozen peaches or other fruit

Place in blender. Add ice to fill. Blend.

A suggestion: Couple your smoothie with this recipe for granola for a "farmer's breakfast" of today.

Cherry Granola

(Serve this tasty treat for breakfast or use it as a topping for yogurt or ice cream.)

4 C old-fashioned oats, uncooked
½ C coarsely chopped pecans
½ C sunflower kernels
¾ C honey
6 tbsp. butter or margarine, melted
1 tsp. vanilla extract
¾ tsp. ground cinnamon
2 C dried tart cherries

Preheat oven to 350°.

Combine oats, pecans, and sunflower kernels in a large bowl. Combine honey, melted butter, vanilla, and cinnamon. Pour over oat mixture, and stir until all dry ingredients are well-coated. Do not add cherries until after it's baked.

Spread mixture on a cookie sheet. Bake in oven at 350° for 30 to 40 minutes or until golden, stirring mixture every ten minutes with spatula. Remove from oven. Stir in cherries. Cool mixture completely. Store tightly covered at room temperature for up to 1 week. Makes 8 cups.

Recipe courtesy of Cherry Marketing Institute

This poem by Rebecca Emlinger Roberts about her parents' honeymoon suggests the passionate beginnings of many cherry country families.

Honeymoon: Torch Lake, Summer 1936

for my mother and father

Rebecca Emlinger Roberts

Imagine green fire,
the lake, burning with sun.
Imagine the irony of love,
the sweat and heat of cherry-picking.
Imagine my parents, so young.

The trick is to guess
how many rungs they'll climb: *They call it*
milking the limb. Ready! Begin!
Fill every bag. Descend.
Pour. Climb. Do it all again.

They pitched their marriage tent
down by the lake: water versus fire.
Lap-lap of desire.
How could they go wrong?

But this is not about the newly
wed, nor the generosity of night in lovers' time.
This is daylight, the Great Depression, tally
of fruit by the dime, the plain good luck of paid labor.

They were beautiful.
Cherries falling through the trees.
Cherries everywhere.

In a minute of an afternoon,
flames consumed their tent.
Picked the tent clean, licked up
what could not be redeemed:
The wedding dress, everything,
except the rings.

Cinders flying through the air. Cinders everywhere.

Who were they, so alive?
Transformed, till I no longer recognize
their silhouettes, lovebirds,
running hands through cold ash,
kissing the nest goodbye.
The lake: bottomless, unfathomable.

40

Water stands for memory; fire for destiny,
tiny ruptures of a bigger flame,
moving toward them, without rancor, toward
fruita de los suenos, fruit of dreams.

---

*The poet thanks the early Mexican migrant workers in the cherry orchards Up North, who
called the cherries *fruita de los suenos*— "fruit of dreams."

Celebration time. . .

Photo of David Fredrickson courtesy of Jim Fredrickson

If everything falls into place as it should, harvest begins approximately the second week of July for tart cherries, with the third week being peak for both sweets and tarts. It is an often heard complaint that there are no local cherries available for National Cherry Festival goers. This has not always been the case.

The National Cherry Festival is now held consistently from the first Saturday of July through the following Saturday. About twenty years ago the festival dates were changed to coincide with the Fourth of July holiday festivities, to draw crowds and ease the schedules of a larger demographic of consumers. What had formerly been a harvest festival became a large moneymaker for the region.

While the festival is a terrific boon to the area financially, industry involvement has unfortunately become limited as a result of the change in date; it's hard to celebrate when you're bringing in a crop, working around the clock, and hoping that all goes well until the process is complete. The only fireworks most cherry industry workers get to see are on the insides of their eyelids when there's time enough to sleep.

During the occasional year when local cherries come in time for Festival, it's a huge logistical nightmare to get semis hauling flatbed or refrigerated trailers through the Parkway coming and going from the orchards. Those are the years when people encounter intersections flooded by cherries that have fallen onto the hot asphalt.

Warren Deering once told me about a more dramatic flood of cherries. A farmer he knew in the 1960's had a full load on and was heading west up the hill from the Parkway on M-72 when his trailer brakes failed. The trailer rolled downhill, spilling its entire load of cherries into the bay.

An imaginative take on such a scene comes from Evalyn Torrant.

ACHOO!

Evalyn Torrant

42

Now Harry wuz a truckin' man
And cherries wuz his load.
He wuz haulin' 'em to New York State
Along a bumpy road
When all at once he had to sneeze
His sneezing gave him fits.
He wrecked his rig and now his load
Ain't cherries, it's the pits.

The National Cherry Festival originated in 1923 as a blessing of the blossoms, patterned after the annual event in Washington DC. The Washington event commemorates the gift in 1912 of 3000 cherry trees by Mayor Yukio Ozaki of Tokyo as a memorial of national friendship between the US and Japan. For many years the local blessing in Northern Michigan was held at Bowers Harbor on Old Mission Peninsula. On a Sunday in May, when blossoms were at their fullest, area clergy and local residents gathered in an area orchard to pray for the success of the cherry crop.

In 1925, the first queen for the festival in Traverse City was chosen. At this time, beauty contests were almost unknown in much of the nation. The event evolved into an annual harvest festival and was declared a national event. It was formally named the National Cherry Festival in 1928. Since then, the festival has been a wonderful annual celebration except for the WWII era years 1942-1947, which were without festivities because of a strong sense of nationalism and the rationing of many consumer goods. Today the week long event features over 120 activities and attracts up to a half million visitors to the area.

Mickey Mouse, Bob Hope, President Gerald Ford, and even the Budweiser Clydesdales have made appearances at the festival in Traverse City. No wonder it has been rated in the top 100 Festivals & Events in North America by the American Business Association and listed often in the top ten events by *USA Today*. And one of the best known dignitaries at the National Cherry Festival is, logically, Mr. Cherry. One day poet MaryAnn Samyn saw him on parade.

Wallace Stevens, Mr. Cherry; Mr. Cherry, Wallace Stevens

MaryAnn Samyn

i.
A man in a suit approaches,
and with him, a bobble of *oh no*.
He is shaped like a bauble, too,
rare jewel for the finger of a giant
or a giant's true love.

ii.
I had gotten brave on the cherries'
tart example,
but when he rounded the corner,
ambled into view. . .

iii.
A carnival mouth gapes in one tent:
win your prize here, girls and ladies.
And chocolate-covered cherries
for all who enter.

iv.
Of course I've got civic pride:
our small town grown up.
Remember when it was all orchard
and your hand was the hand
that did the reaching?

v.
July. The month itself ripens
and flares like our sunsets
or our cherried lips.

vi.
As a metaphor, he's good.
as a pie, he might be even better.

vii.
This time of year, our preference
is a given, like the undulating
rows of trees, or the shoreline
that shifts and stays the same.

viii.
The Queen in her convertible
and the loop of her sash:
what goes around comes around:
the cherry and the pit of the cherry.

xi.
His hands, white gloves, correspond
to nothing so much
as our state itself, its greeting
and *come back soon*, its palm
where we rest, its little finger.

x.
But when it was done,
there was the idea of all winter,
cold like the juice we drank
to tide us over.

One day in May of 2005, I pulled my June *Reader's Digest* from my mailbox. Leafing through it on the way into the house, I discovered that the festival had again made news as something important and enjoyable to do when visiting the Midwest. Posted beside the blurb was a version of a recipe for cherry fruit crunch from the Gregory family in Suttons Bay, Michigan. I couldn't believe it—this was from people I know locally! "Lu," the recipe's inventor, is Bob and Don Gregory's mother, Luella Gregory; the brothers run Cherry Bay Orchards, Inc., in Suttons Bay, Michigan.

Lu's Cherry Fruit Crunch

For crust:

1 C butter
2 C flour
1½ C brown sugar
½ C slivered chopped almonds

For filling:

1 pt. whipping cream
1 C powdered sugar
8 oz. cream cheese, softened

For topping:
4 C sweet cherries, pitted
¾ C sugar
¼ C cornstarch
1 C water
½ tsp. almond extract

Preheat oven to 400°. Combine all ingredients for crust, press into 9" x 13" baking pan. Bake for 15 minutes; cool.

For filling, whip cream and add sugar; fold in cream cheese. Spread on top of cooled crust. REFRIGERATE.

For topping, combine cherries and sugar in saucepan over medium heat. Whisk cornstarch into water then add to cherries and sugar in saucepan. Stir to remove lumps. Cook until thick. Stir in extract. Let it cool. Then spread over cheese mixture in crust; chill. Makes 20 bars.

(You may substitute Montmorency Tart or Balaton cherries for dark sweets, or if unavailable or under time constraints, use a can of tart cherry pie filling.)

Recipe courtesy of the Gregory family

To become the National Cherry Queen is a great honor. The young lady selected for the job is expected to travel nationally and internationally, to promote not only the festival itself but the cherry industry and the region. She is apt to ride elephants, be kissed by "Sparty," and make gifts of pies to political figures. There are scholarship awards for the participating finalists of over $12,500 at the time of this writing, underwritten by area sponsors. Making appearances is a crucial part of the queen's responsibilities. Her ability and effectiveness in representing the industry will affect how she is remembered.

Maggie Schneider, Cherry Queen of 2004, will be remembered especially for her resilience. In November of 2004, she was in an automobile accident which forced her to struggle not only with the responsibilities of her reign, but with the basics of physical movement. She was hospitalized for nearly two months. She learned the virtue of patience as she relearned how to walk and regained the use of her hands. Though she missed out on participating in the Rose Bowl during her reign, she did have quite an adventure with the crew of The Learning Channel's show *Trading Spaces*. In June 2005 the show filmed in Traverse City, featuring the home of Jennifer Buell. Miss Schneider appeared on the episode to give a pie and other cherry products to one of the show's carpenters, Carter Oosterhouse, who is a TC native.

Industry involvement is still a priority for former queens Kelsey (Hewitt) LaCross of 2001's festival and Sara McGuire, who won in 1995 when she was Sara Veliquette. Kelsey is now part of the LaCross family, cherry growers and processors. Sara and her husband Patrick own and operate Royal Farms, Inc., in Ellsworth, Michigan. Their business was named for her reign as queen shortly before the two married. Here is one of Sara's recipes.

Ginger-Spiced Cherries—a relish

1 16 oz. can dark sweet cherries
2 tbsp. of sugar
1 tbsp. cornstarch
1 tbsp. candied ginger, thinly sliced
2 tsp. lemon juice

Drain cherries, reserving juice; add water if needed, to make 1 cup of liquid.

Mix a small amount of cherry juice and cornstarch. Combine with the rest of the cherry juice, lemon juice, sugar, and ginger. Cook until clear and thick; add cherries. Serve cold as a meat accompaniment.

Recipe courtesy of Sara (Veliquette) McGuire, National Cherry Festival Queen, 1995

Coronation balls, parades, meetings with celebrities, and being celebrated as queen for the National Cherry Festival are lifetime memories for the young women who have graced our region as queens or members of the court. But to me the idea of royalty extends elsewhere. The young women of migrant families who come to our area every summer to work in the industry are the real queens. But their celebrations and opportunities for honor differ from the region's older traditions.

The coming-of-age celebration called the "quinceañara," held when a girl reaches her fifteenth birthday, is widespread in Latin-American culture. The word stems from the Spanish quince for "fifteen" and años for "years." The origins are often attributed to the ancient customs of the Aztecs, although many cultures have similar traditions. Fifteen was the age when many girls traditionally passed into womanhood, marrying and starting a family. So the celebration was of great importance.

Nowadays the quinceañara usually symbolizes that a young woman is old enough to date. For the event a grand gown is chosen, musicians are hired, and a feast is laid. All of this costs about as much as a wedding would. It is traditional for the parents of the young girl to have the help of sponsors or "padrinos" for different parts of the party. I first learned of the tradition when my husband and I were asked by a couple I worked with to be padrinos for their daughter's celebration. I was extremely flattered that they considered us to be like part of their family. Since then we have had the honor of being padrinos for two other young ladies.

The quinceañara has two parts—the mass and the fiesta. The most symbolic act during the festivities is the changing of the shoes. During the mass a little boy carries a pillow with the birthday girl's shoes, while a little girl carries a pillow with a tiara for her. At the fiesta, the girl's mother dances with her and then takes her to a make-believe throne and crowns her with the tiara. Then the girl's father switches her shoes, from flats to her first pair of high heels, and he dances with her; his own princess.

The tradition has become considerably Americanized; as people have begun to assimilate, often their historical and cultural traditions are left by the wayside. Some girls still celebrate the quinceañara as a form of "Sweet Sixteen" party. There's still the crown, the gown, and the party. Although it is difficult in some regions to be able to fully celebrate the tradition, St. Michael's Church in Suttons Bay and Immaculate Conception Church in Traverse City hold training classes for the girls to fulfill their requirement for the celebration's mass to be held in their honor. After their training, they can truly be queen for a day.

Martha and Mayra Martinez, and Jessica Garza are shown here in their quinceañara gowns.

Getting to work. . .

Photo of cars near migrant housing, 1966-67, courtesy of Jim Fredrickson

The earliest commercial cherry crops, between the 1910's and 1960's, were all hand harvested by migrant pickers. Finding a place that paid a good wage was difficult during the Depression era and the war years. Workers rode the trains up to Northern Michigan en masse. Back then, migrants were not automatically assumed to be Hispanic. Migrants were nomads, and could be Irish, Scottish or Bohemian immigrants, former lumber workers of Scandinavian descent, descendents of freed slaves, failed sharecroppers, etc. The literal definition of migrant worker was, and is, simply people who move from one region to another to find work.

The cherry region, like commercial agriculture everywhere in the U.S., relies heavily upon its migrant worker population. In Northern Michigan during the spring, phone lines are burning up with calls for cherry harvest worker recruitment. Mostly, it's a matter of calling the families who have been coming to the region for years, to ask them if they'll be returning for the season. Working long hours together for a common goal, getting in the crop, and earning a living together also cultivate friendships.

Photo of migrants riding on freight cars, early 1930's, courtesy of Leelanau Historical Museum

I'm happy to say that, in my experience, many companies in the cherry industry value and promote mutual respect between administration and the crews the industry depends upon. In many areas of the country, migrant labor is exploited and considered expendable; compassion and respect for people are often lacking. Often wage scales are low, and turnover is high; as a result, overall production is negatively affected. I'm grateful that the companies I've worked with care about their crews.

52

For example, when my boss started the migrant housing camp on the plant's premises, his philosophy was that the camp should be designed so that it would be comfortable and acceptable should a member of administration need to live there. I didn't realize the poor living conditions some workers face until I had a conversation with a Michigan Department of Agriculture regional camp inspector. I learned that some places still have community outdoor plumbing, have no heating, and are not well-maintained. Since the need for labor is usually seasonal, many camp owners are unwilling to invest in making their camps decent places to live.

Another important philosophy in the companies where I've worked is the concept that if you are in an administrative position, you shouldn't expect others to do what you are unwilling to do yourself. This is important in building a strong production crew that works well together. Trust and respect are important parts of running a successful crew.

Migrant crews and families follow the fruit and vegetable harvest, moving gradually north through the year as crops become ready. Michigan harvests begin with blueberries in southern Michigan, moving up the coast of Lake Michigan to asparagus and strawberries, then cherries, then heading south again for picking the pickling cucumbers, then carrots. Autumn brings them back north again for apples and then back to the South for sugar beets and tomatoes. Finally, for winter they go to work the citrus regions and onion fields.

To some, the nomadic way of life is necessary. More often than not, workers who come to Northern Michigan are supporting numerous family members who've remained at home. They send home most of their earnings, usually keeping just enough for living and travel expenses. But when that runs out and the next crop isn't quite ready, there's little to live on before the next paycheck. Area agencies such as Telamon Corp. in Traverse City, and other human service agencies try to assist incoming families. But with cuts to federal and state funding, there are fewer places to turn for help.

The Traverse City area has the benefit of good-hearted people and a growing Hispanic ministry which helps our migrant population in many ways in times of need. With the leadership *53* of Rev. Wayne Dziekan, his pastoral associate Gladys Munoz, Fr. Rey Garcia, and Silvia Cortes, the ministry is a vital part of the community. They help to find work, housing, and funds for families, celebrate weekly bilingual mass at St. Michael's Church, minister at area migrant camps, and even assist families who have lost a loved one, helping to get their departed back home and offering counseling to the family. The ministry has a program for young people from throughout the Northern Michigan diocese, arranging for them to visit fruit farms, processing facilities, and camps to gain a better understanding of the migrant way of life. Students have traveled to Mexico's border towns for the past several years as part of the "Borderlinks" program. Last summer a combined Anglo/Hispanic celebration with traditional Mexican cuisine, music, and dancing was held to further integrate the community.

The following article was written in the summer of 1996 by Juan A. Marinez, who works for Michigan State University's College of Agriculture and Cooperative Extension Service. He is currently doing research on the growth in the number of Mexican farm owners in Michigan, including factors that lead to their being undercounted. Juan also does USDA liaison work for the College on grants and policy. This article previously appeared on a website for literature of indigenous peoples compiled by Glen Welker.

Fields of Dreams

Migrant worker Erica Sanchez wants her world to go beyond the cherry farms of Michigan's Suttons Bay.

Erica Sanchez has been picking cherries since second grade, since the day her father decided she was old and strong enough to strap a pail around her neck and go to work with her family.

She is 22 now, with goals and dreams far loftier than the cherry trees of Leelanau County. She cannot begin to estimate the number of cherries that passed through her small hands. Yet even after 14 years, she will stop sometimes and look at a single cherry cradled in her palm.

At that instant—those few seconds in a hot, dirty day— "I feel special," Sanchez says. She'll notice the curves of the cherry, the shades of red and the spots of yellow or green, and she'll think, "Hey, I picked this cherry. Maybe Madonna will eat it, or President Clinton."

Five months a year, her world is a migrant camp and the fields and orchards around it. At the same time, her world and her pride have no limit. She is proud of her father, who used to ride his bicycle across the border from Mexico to work in the fields. Of her mother, who rises at 5 a.m. to make the tortillas the family will eat for lunch. Of her older sister, Christina, a nursing student. And of her high school diploma and plans to become a schoolteacher and her vision of summers spent helping the migrant children who remind her of herself.

Sanchez, her parents, her two brothers, and two younger sisters left the southern tip of Texas a month ago in a 1983 Dodge van. In Suttons Bay, 17 miles north of Traverse City, they live a familiar routine: the strawberry harvest, then cherries, then apples as the weather turns and they begin to head for home.

A long winter and cool spring pushed back the strawberry harvest and will delay the beginning of cherry season to next week at the earliest. For the first time Sanchez can remember, none of her cherries will grace the National Cherry Festival, which ends its eight-day run Saturday in Traverse City.

Sanchez has never been to the festival, which brings 500,000 people to the northwest corner of the Michigan mit- *55* ten. She has never seen the bands and floats and Budweiser Clydesdales of the Cherry Royale Parade, or eaten at the Sara Lee Cherry Pie Pavilion, or watched a free concert at the bay-front bandstand.

But even as the festival imports 30,000 pounds of fresh cherries from Washington, it acknowledges a bond with Sanchez. For all the heavy machines rumbling through orchards at harvest times, she and a few thousand other migrant workers remain the literal backbone of the industry.

Migrants hand-pick virtually all the sweet cherries, the ones that go directly from carton to mouth. After mechanical tree-shakers drop tart cherries from other trees onto tarpaulins, migrants hold the heavy tarps while the machines pull the cherries onto conveyor belts. Migrants sort cherries at processing plants and spray pesticides. And once in a while, a migrant might hold a round, ripe, perfect cherry in the palm of her hand and wonder at it all.

Sanchez holds out her arms to Carina Barrajas, and the curly-haired 11-month old climbs into her lap and stops squalling. Carina is the daughter of a family friend who bunks in another camp. It's a few days before the beginning of strawberry season and the migrants, idle for two weeks, are running out of ways to fill time. Sanchez is tending Carina in the crowded living room of an elderly mobile home. She is good with babies, good with all kids. In fact, two years ago she was a teacher aid at a summer migrant school and day care center.

This summer, she will work mostly with fruit, either picking or sorting it. On fortunate days, she may be assigned to baby-sit. But her father tells her all the time to work toward something else. It's the American Dream, outlined in Spanish. *Get an education. Be somebody. Do better than your parents.*

Domingo Sanchez Sr. was born in the United States, but he and his wife, Eleuteria, grew up in Mexico. Neither speaks English.

For the three older kids, points out Erica Sanchez, "There was nobody to help us with our homework." The three youngest have been luckier, getting educational hand-me-downs from their siblings, but they still have to switch schools every fall when the family drives the 1,800 miles back to Elsa, Texas.

Sanchez's English is accented but grammatically solid, an odd advantage learning it exclusively at school. Confident and outgoing, she has evolved into the family spokeswoman. When the Sanchez's wanted to bring friends to work this year, Erica dialed up the president of Cherry Bay Orchards. Don Gregory said, "Sure bring 'em up." The Sanchez's have worked for him eight years, and he trusts them. Besides, he wouldn't want to disappoint her, "Everyone likes Erica," Gregory says. She is the life of what passes for party; regardless of who she's working with, she'll joke around with them. "A little playfulness," explains Sanchez "helps people forget how much their muscles ache. You have to be there, so you might as well try to make it fun."

She does not look to be cut out for field work. With her high cheekbones and rounded face, she seems too young to drive, let alone work a seven-day week. Were this a workday, she would be wearing a baseball cap over her shoulder-length hair and long sleeves to protect her arms from pesticides. Instead, she chose a short-sleeved black top, black print slacks, and backless espadrilles. On her right middle finger is her ring from Edcouch-Elsa High School. She could not afford a gemstone, so the center of the ring is clear glass. In the glass is the school mascot, the industrious bee.

The reward for years of good work and loyalty is the best trailer in the camp. Five mobile homes squat on one side of a grass and gravel cul-de-sac surrounded by towering maples. A chain of clotheslines stretches the length of the oval drive. The Sanchez home, the last of the cluster, sits parallel to the gravel road. Two bench-style car seats out front serve as lawn chairs.

Erica Sanchez and her sisters Diana, 13, and Brenda, 10, share one bedroom. Their parents get the other. Domingo Jr., 21 and Jose Miguel, 18, sleep on sofas in the living room, where the door is open to an early afternoon breeze.

"This is heaven for us, for camp to be like this," Erica Sanchez says. Others in the living room nod. Some migrants have to sleep in tents. Others sleep in their cars. "We've stayed where the shower is outside, the bathroom is outside. Everything is outside."

The Sanchez's have a television and a stereo old enough that it uses a turntable. They had a phone two summers ago but took it out after Erica ran up a $200 bill calling friends in Elsa. To the left of the television, stacked next to the door, are four fresh tires for the van.

Jose Miguel is parked across from the tires, playing a video game on the TV set with Robert Orozco. Jose Miguel is in a recliner, and Robert, a 14-year-old camp neighbor, is slouched across the mismatched ottoman. He's wearing a black Michael Jordan uniform top. Diana and Brenda are riding herd on a 3-year-old girl and 8-month-old boy the children of another camp neighbor. Domingo Sr. is watching the video game and Eleuteria is watching everything.

"Strawberries are the worst," Erica says, and again there is agreement in the room. "You have to bend down all day. You get home and you're all red. You even smell like a strawberry."

The only good thing about strawberry season is that it means that cherries are coming. All harvests pay roughly the same, about $250 a week after taxes for a good picker. But cherries are easier. There is more variety to the work and the fruit tastes terrific right off the tree.

"I can eat cherries all day and all night," Sanchez says, smiling at the thought. Workers can take cherries home, and they tend to eat them until their bodies beg for mercy.

"You going to get sick this year?" Jose Miguel asks Robert.

Robert, busy killing futuristic gladiators, does not take his eyes from TV screen. "Yep."

In the early 1960's, before automation, northwest Michigan growers needed 35,000 migrants to get the crops in. Local restaurants served blue-plate Mexican dinners on Thursday night. On weekends, Spanish-language movies were projected onto the outside wall of a store in Suttons Bay.

The industry gets by nowadays with 4,500 migrants, many of whom work only during apple season. A dead-end job has become deader.

By the time the younger girls finish high school, the Sanchez's may have given up the road. Christina will be a nurse. Domingo Jr. has trained to paint cars. Domingo Sr., who built the family's small home in Elsa, is slowly working on a larger one with four bedrooms, two baths—and he says that when it is finished, so is he.

Only Erica plans to keep coming north.

She has found her calling and her college, Pan American University of Edinburg, Texas. She has not found the money to go there, but she says with absolute certainty that she will.

She will become Miss Sanchez the schoolteacher, and when her students go home for the summer, she will go to Suttons Bay. She will work with migrant children, she says, teaching them to read and dream. And every year, on a bright July Saturday, they will all go to the cherry festival parade.

Juan A. Marinez

59

Photo, c. 1890, courtesy of Benzie Area Historical Society

Whether by Dodge van, horse-drawn wagonload, or other means, getting to work and getting through the day and the season have always been uppermost in the minds of those involved in the cherry industry. During harvest, as I drive up Indian Hill Road toward Empire, I imagine my brother on the same road in the 1970's, flying downhill on his 10-speed bike before he bought his first truck with earnings from working a "cherry pack."

The world is a different place before sunrise. It's eerie, as well as austerely beautiful. The deer move in pre-dawn's protection, so I roll my windows down, blasting Aerosmith or a Vivaldi concerto at superstitious decibels to warn them. The chill of the morning air is bracing. It helps me wake up, along with a super-sized Mountain Dew from the all-night gas station.

One morning on that drive, I found a black handmade man's hat with a maker's mark inside sitting at the side of the road at the intersection of M-22 and Fowler Road as if it had landed from the night sky. All that fall I tried unsuccessfully to track down the hat's owner. I've kept it as a souvenir because it had been an omen. That was the day that I had to call St. Michael's Church in Suttons Bay to help a family on our crew who had lost one of their members to suicide during the night.

Summer nights have the potential to change us somehow.

The Silence That Follows

Gerry LaFemina

It's early summer in Grayling, & death has no business here
despite my neighbor celebrating his 93rd June.
Black flies convene above
                      the ruffled surface of the AuSable
while adolescents dream of canoeing toward Wakely Bridge
with dates or their fathers. On street corners

the stands are up, some selling cherry bombs & rockets,
some selling Old Mission cherries. I knew a young woman,
yes, years ago, who could twist
                      cherry stems into knots
with her tongue, & what young man wouldn't love that?
All I could do was spit the pits of those tart fruits

& never far enough to win a ribbon at Cherry Fest.
All I could do was tell her *I love you*, but
there was no ribbon for that, either.
                      Still, I'll stop my car
along the shoulder of West 72, buy a pound of cherries
& admire their merlot bodies, their skin

taut & rounded. I could be in love all over again
with the scent of fresh cherries. When it ended
there was nothing our tongues could do,
                      no words we might tie
together to make anything all right. Her name translates
into *I love* or *I like*. I lived three blocks from Mercy Hospital then

though there was no mercy to be had that long August
in the empty bag of our house. I sat & listened
to ambulances rushing in.
                      The siren howled like a lonely man
or like a lonely woman. It's early summer in Grayling,
& I have three dollars worth of cherries, & I never did learn

how she did that trick with her tongue & the stem,
though I used to finger those knots like a Persian
reading a rug. Translation's
                           such a subjective art. I'd say
her name twice in a row—*I like   I like*—
& now I've stopped saying it at all, & stopped even

thinking of her. Tonight I'll eat Michigan cherries from brown
        paper
& from my porch watch an ambulance hurry with its charges.
Behind it, a car full of prayers.
                           In the silence that follows
I might hear the river only a block away:
a quick splashing of something crossing over to the near shore.

Upon arrival at the processing plant, I start doing the record keeping for the previous night crew's production, setting up paperwork and codes for day shift's run, checking and stocking production supplies, starting the first 30-cup pot of coffee in the break-room, and putting out any metaphorical fires so the day will run smoothly. This is before the day crew arrives, often before the night crew departs. I'm usually there when the night crew arrives for their shift, too. The most hours I ever clocked in a week was 102; that was with a day off on Sunday.

62

The summer moon fades into beautiful sunrises. If there's enough time to glance out the window and gulp some coffee before starting a new task, it is a moment of grace. During one of these moments, I learned about the coronas sometimes seen around the moon. One summer a clean-up crew worker taught me the word's significance: corona is Spanish (and also Latin) for wreath, halo or crown. He told me he also saw them over Lake Michigan when he worked in the clothing district in Chicago. Sometimes they formed "moon dogs," bright spots in the ice clouds on either side of the moon.

Trucks arrive through the night loaded with cherry tanks. Maximum capacity for a flatbed trailer is 32 tanks, or approximately

32,000 pounds. It's not unusual to receive 200,000 pounds per shift. And we're always trying to increase processing capacity.

The tanks are then unloaded onto the cooling pad where water is pumped through the tanks. A hydro-cooler system lowers the water temp to about 36 degrees Fahrenheit, just above freezing. It is critical to get the cherries cool before running them through the pitting and sorting lines so the fruit will be firm and retain its quality throughout the processing time. Often the cold water and the rising sun's heat create fog on the pad, giving another atmospheric personality to the morning.

For many years, the common practice was to can cherries in industrial Number 10 cans, lined to prevent corrosion. They were sold primarily to bakeries and for government contracts for schools and prisons.

Most cannery equipment has been discarded in recent years due to marketing trend changes. Local tart cherries these days are usually packed for the drying pool. That means they are packed in 5-gallon plastic pails for IQF (Individual Quick Frozen) processing. They are stored in freezers and then trucked to drying facilities to become dried cherries for retail and wholesale markets.

During the first "pack" I worked, when we were still canning, I had several 36" industrial fans delivered the first day of production and was giving out electrolyte tablets to the crew because the cookers put out so much heat. When we stopped canning cherries in 2000, the removal of the large cookers and other canning equipment made the workplace a more comfortable environment. Temperatures in the processing plant are 20-30 degrees cooler now during tart cherry harvest production, even in full operation. During the "off season," there's room for setting up bottling equipment for cherry concentrate and more tanks for preparing maraschino cherries.

"Cherry pack" is an endurance test that lasts anywhere from two to five weeks. To get crews for day and night shifts filled is not easy. But once the key roles are filled, things begin to fall into place. Especially for quality assurance staff, equipment operators, supervisors (preferably with translation skills), but really for every position, it is essential to assign the right personnel. It is important to be able to read people and to know their experience and their capabilities. Orientations, training sessions, and trial runs are all a part of it, too. This allows for placement of workers so that everyone will get along together, apply their abilities, work within the parameters of good manufacturing procedures, and follow compliance guidelines. The result will be fine quality end-products.

Photo courtesy of Jim Fredrickson

When the last tank of cherries is emptied into the hopper of the de-stemmer unit and they roll up the conveyors into the last pails to be filled, there is admittedly a huge sigh of relief and cause for celebration. Usually, I've completed all but the final tally for the final code for the final run report when I allow myself the possibility of thinking of a proper night's sleep. I remember a few summers ago, when the last load of product was signed for by the driver we called "the old Crow"; I doubt that I will ever see a bigger smile than his, as he headed out for the freezers in his truck.

This sentiment is shared by many who've just finished getting in the crop. A light-hearted poem by industry leader Norm Veliquette reflects such a sense of relief.

After the Pack

Norman Veliquette

The cooling pad is dry
And the fire has gone out.
No forklift trucks whining,
No supervisor's shout.

The harvest tanks are stacked
And the orchard grass is tall.
The cherries rest in darkness,
No sugar trucks to call.

The days were long and hard,
Nights I do not remember.
A school bus goes by.
It must be September.

66

The pies have it...

Cherry Pie

Conrad Hilberry

We're all acquainted with the airy
crowd—a stalk of celery dipped
in cottage cheese, a thimble

of soy milk, a few green grapes.
I invite them over here: between
two butter crusts, my sour

flesh so deeply sugared it
astounds the mouth.
To coax it all to bed, a downy

pillow of whipped cream.
Try me, you organics.
Light the oven.

Let me show you how
the juices leap, when nature
shares the sheets with art.

"It's as American as apple pie" should be changed to *cherry pie*. Or at least they should share the title representative of home, comfort, and nostalgia. Mottos aside, one of Northern Michigan's most notable cherry pie bakeries is The Cherry Hut Restaurant in Beulah, Michigan. Their easily recognized smiling faced logo, "Cherry Jerry," has been trademarked by its current manager Andrew Case and shines down on us from Memorial Day weekend through late October. They're kept busy baking and serving 300-400 pies each day, topping 500 in the peak weeks of summer. The recipe is consistent with their history; it hasn't changed since 1922, even with remodeling jobs and updates. They've maintained their identity, their homey All-American menu and quality of service, and the feeling that everything's right with the world when you lay down your fork.

Cherry Hut photos (c. 1922 and c. 1950) courtesy of Andrew Case.

The Cherry Hut has been featured in *LIFE* magazine, *The New York Times*, *USA Today*, the *Indianapolis Star*, and *People* Magazine. They also have been spotlighted in many travel guides for dining, especially because of their pie. Their cherry pie! Who would have thought that a pie-stand started on the north shore of Crystal Lake by the Kraker family in 1922 would come to such acclaim, withstanding the ever-changing world we live in?

My first job ever was at The Cherry Hut. It was a challenge to find the required black and white saddle shoe oxfords (Golden Shoes on Front Street in Traverse City was the only place that carried them), and to pedal my bike to work every day the summer of my fifteenth year. But it was fun. The girls I worked with became my friends, and we still maintain contact after more than twenty years. I returned there to work other summers, referring to my bright red pinafore dress and crisp white blouse as my "costume." I was drawn back because there was a sense of family, and the customers who returned every summer and watched us grow into adulthood were always wonderful.

Leonard Case (Andrew's dad) has kept all of the old menus with the names of servers and bakers printed on the back for posterity. A former dishwasher and pie-baker is now a well-respected local optometrist. One of my good friends from that first summer now works for FEMA and the Secret Service. Another has been a teacher in battle-torn Iraq. Some have gone on to greater fame: I believe Mary Gross from Saturday Night Live worked there as a kid.

I had the privilege of meeting another notable pie-baker at a friend's barbeque down on the Platte River. Her name is Mary Weider and she told me how she loves to bake. She's in her 90's now, and when she was awarded a prize for her cherry pie by the Cherryland Electric Cooperative, she had to have a driver take her to the contest (as well as to the BBQ). Mary is a naturalized U.S. citizen who was born in Switzerland. Her family fled to Italy during WWI, but was captured and placed in a refugee camp. After the war she returned to Italy and then came to the Detroit area, where she married and then moved to Northern Michigan. Her family has always said she makes the best pies, and now she has proof of it.

69

Another noteworthy source for pie is Cherry Republic in Glen Arbor, where they tout True Cherry Pie made the old-fashioned way, using tapioca as a thickening agent. Pie is served daily, and customers can take one home with them. They also offer jars of whole and sliced tart cherries sweetened just the right amount, for customers to take home for home-baking.

Pie-baking has different associations and memories for different people.

The Edge

Rhoda Janzen

Picked and stemmed; trained
my thumb to blunt the knife so that
I pitted with an aunt's concentration;

tucked sour cherries into sugar;
eked almond like a story, lapped
little pats of butter, pinch-cheeked;

sealed without tearing the edge.
Cherry pie-by-the-yard
looked like a long white fish

To be divided among multitudes.
the crust, light or heavy,
savvy as the many moods

of guilt, could trust and obey
the need, O the church mouth
when, amazed by grace, they

stood to sing. Smell of chins
and casseroles, powdery squeezes
on the upper arm. Mrs. Lorenze

bent over me, robust, perfumed.
On her shoulder sat a phoenix
with a golden eye that bloomed

Stern above the social perms.
No thank you, ma'am, but already
one of those summer storms

had cut the darkening sky like sin.
Clouds crimped the sky. I heard
distant thunder of a rolling pin.

The following recipe was contributed by Marjory Veliquette of Elk Rapids, who says that when she was a young girl, she and her friends always used this recipe when they wanted to place well in a baking contest. Marjory is part of Great Lakes Packing Company and has been involved in many aspects of the cherry industry through the years.

Mother Mac's Cherry Pie

¼ C sugar
Dash of salt
3 tbsp. cornstarch
¼ C cherry juice (not concentrate)
¾ C sugar
½ C cherry juice
2 C tart cherries, canned or frozen (drained)
¼ tsp. lemon or almond extract
¼ tsp. red food coloring
2 tbsp. of butter
Crust for a 2-crust pie (see next recipe or use frozen)

Preheat oven to 375°. Mix ¼ cup sugar, salt, and cornstarch. Add ¼ cup cherry juice to make a paste. In a saucepan mix ¾ cup sugar and ½ cup cherry juice and bring to a boil. When boiling, slowly add the cornstarch mixture. Stir constantly and cook until thick and clear. Fold in the cherries and add the lemon or almond extract, food coloring, and butter. Pour into pie crust, cover with top crust and bake at 375° for 1 hour.

E.Z. Pie Crust

1½ C flour
½ C oil
½ tsp. salt
2 tbsp. milk
3 tbsp. sugar

Mix all ingredients. Double amount for 2 crusted
pie—divide and roll half to fit top of pie to cover. Press
bottom half into pie dish, fill with pie filling
prepared or any filling desired. Cover with other half of
pastry. Crimp and trim edges. Vent top for baking.

Recommended pastry crust recipe by Marjory Veliquette from her friend E.Z. Martineau

Cherry pie is all about nostalgia. My grandmother used to sing,
"Can she bake a cherry pie, Billy boy, Billy boy? Can she bake
a cherry pie, charming Billy?" In times of great upheaval and
worry or even in times of contented joy, it can be a comfort to
bake something distinctly wonderful for those we love.

Sour Pie Cherries

Barbara Crooker

I.

Blue envelope.
The letter's come from Florida,
as I knew it would, soon
after your last one telling
how his heart kept stopping,
how the machines couldn't keep him
much longer. You were married
fifty-seven years.

II.

Today it's the height of June,
and I'm picking sour cherries
to put by for pies.
Here in the north,
they need that snow
to run with the juice.
Each red globe pulls away,
flesh from stone
only when ripe;
such sweetness in our bodies,
what's sure, what's tangible.

III.

At the sink, I push the pits
out with my thumb.
How did this fruit come
from such small flowers,
delicate lace,
spring snow drifting
from bough to bough?

IV.

I am making pie crust,
cutting lard into flour and salt;
the floor is white with flurries.
Whatever cracks can be pinched and patched.
I stir the cherries with sugar and butter,
a bowlful of garnets shines in the pan.
Fancy with lattice-work, crimped-in designs,
I make this in his memory,
your life and mine, the tart, the bitter, the sweet.

Each tart cherry tree produces about 7000 cherries. Approximately 250 cherries are needed for a cherry pie. One slow afternoon at "The Hut," the pie-baker and dishwasher on duty and I counted the cherries from three pies. The average number in their pies at that time was 312. It's probably the same today.

Classic Cherry Pie

This classic recipe is sure to please family and friends.

1 package refrigerated pie crust for 9-inch pie
2 (20- or 21-oz.) cans cherry pie filling
½ tsp. almond extract, optional

Line a 9-inch pie pan with pie crust. Trim crust along pan edge. Pour cherry pie filling evenly into crust. Sprinkle with almond extract, if desired.

Place second crust over filling. Wrap excess top crust under bottom crust. Press edges together with a fork. With a knife, cut slits in top crust.

Bake in a preheated 400-degree oven 35 to 40 minutes, or until crust is golden brown. Cover edge of crust with strips of foil, if needed, to prevent over-browning. Makes 6 to 8 servings.

Note: If desired, I cup of dried tart cherries can be mixed with the cherry filling before baking for added cherry flavor.

Recipe courtesy of Cherry Marketing Institute

74

Participation in the preparation of a meal or special dish can be a rite of passage, as well.

Cherry Pantoum

Pamela Ditchoff

Late Julys of my childhood
Great Aunt Dot and I picked tart Montmorency cherries
From the orchard of her Saint John's farm.
She said, The riper the cherry the sweeter the pie.

Great Aunt Dot and I picked tart Montmorency cherries,
Filled sweet grass baskets to the brim.
She said, The riper the cherry the sweeter the pie,
As we carried cherries to the summer kitchen.

Filled sweet grass baskets to the brim
Set upon the sun warmed pine floor
Ripe scent filling the summer kitchen
Large green bowls in our laps.

Onto the sun warmed pine floor
We dropped stones separated from fruit,
Sweet meat fell into large green bowls in our laps
From our hands, mine smooth as a cherry, hers rough as bark.

Dropped stones separated from fruit,
Montmorency cherries prepared for pies
From our hands, mine smooth as a cherry, hers rough as bark.
When will I be grown, I asked,

As we carried the cherries prepared for pies
Into the kitchen to roll out crusts.
When will I be grown, I asked.
She said, In the twinkling of an eye,
The riper the cherry the sweeter the pie.

76

On top. . .

Photo of crew leader and his crew, courtesy of Jim Fredrickson

From Wikipedia, the free online encyclopedia:

A maraschino cherry is a preserved, sweetened cherry, typically made from light-colored sweet cherries, such as the Royal Ann, Rainier, or Gold varieties. The cherries are first preserved in a brine solution or ethanol, then soaked in a suspension of food coloring, sugar syrup, artificial and natural flavors, and other components. Maraschino cherries dyed red are typically almond-flavored, while cherries dyed green are usually peppermint-flavored.

The name maraschino refers to the marasca cherry and a liqueur made from it, in which maraschino cherries were originally preserved. Originally produced for and consumed as a delicacy by royalty and the wealthy, the cherries were first introduced in the United States in the late 19th century, where they were served in fine restaurants.

By the turn of the century, American producers were experimenting with flavors such as the almond extract used today.

During Prohibition in the United States, Ernest H. Wiegand, a professor of horticulture at Oregon State University, developed the modern method of manufacturing maraschino cherries using a brine solution rather than alcohol. Thus, most modern maraschino cherries have only an historical connection with the liqueur maraschino.

Maraschino cherries are an important ingredient in many cocktails. As a garnish, they often decorate baked ham, pastry, parfaits, ice cream sundaes and ice cream sodas.

Hand-picked light sweet cherries with their stems intact usually become the movie stars of the cherry world—maraschino cherries, destined for a cocktail glass or the top of an ice cream sundae or some other fabulous dessert. However, most light sweets from the region become "dippers" because the orchards use shakers and de-stemmer units for increasing harvest results. These stemless cherries are used to create delectable cherry cordials or are chopped into halves and pieces for ice cream makers.

Most people have heard legends or myths about maraschinos. One myth is that they're preserved in formaldehyde. However, absolutely no formaldehyde is used in making maraschino cherries; that myth may have been started when a writer for a national news magazine confused formaldehyde with benzahdehyde, a flavoring oil extracted from cherry, almond, or walnut pits which is used in the process. It's the same flavor in Dr. Pepper® cola.

Another myth is that the red dye in maraschinos is the one that raised cancer scares in the 1970's. However, Red Dye #3 was the dye that caused health problems; cherry manufacturers use Red Dye #40, the same dye used in chewing gum, egg coloring kits, and some flavored potato chips.

When someone mentions maraschinos or chocolate covered cherries it's hard not to imagine the infamous factory scene from "I Love Lucy," when Lucy is working on the line. But it's not usually that crazy; instead, standing on the line for hours sorting fruit allows the mind to wander in many different directions. One example comes from Judith Kerman's teenage experience in a local candy shop that dipped its own chocolates.

Packing Cherry Cordials

Judith Kerman

A chocolate-covered cherry
seduces the fingertips like gold coins,
slightly greasy, a satin rosebud
smelling of fruit and cocoa butter.
When you hold it like your lover's hand,
you can feel the slight give
of a surface ready to crush.
Your mouth imagines rivers in flood,
the collapse of the chocolate,
the rush of cherry syrup,
sweet fibrous wetness.
In latex gloves
you pluck it from the waxed paper,
deposit it in a frill of dark-brown,
tuck it into a two-pound heart
lined with pink satin.
A crew-cut young man
in a Varsity jacket
will buy it for his girl,
a bottle-blonde cheerleader
with too much makeup.
Or perhaps it's for his mother.

Cherries can be dyed other colors besides bright red. Green cherries are often made for fruitcake bakers. One company that finishes maraschinos for export has created electric blue, yellow, pink, and orange ones. But red is what we know and remember.

Maraschino cherries are not bleached, as many presume. Rather, they begin as a light yellow sweet cherry, usually of the Queen Anne, Rainier, or Napoleon varieties. Then they are pitted, stored in brine, and sold to finish processing plants. At the finishing stage they are washed for a long time to eliminate the brine. Then they are colored, sweetened, and flavored to customer specifications. It takes from five days to two weeks for the batch of maraschinos to become whatever the customer needs, whether they are for ice cream makers, confectioners, or bakeries.

A fun way to "finish" maraschinos at home is to make the following treat.

Chocolate Cherry Bombs

1 (10 oz.) jar of maraschino cherries with stems
2 C vanilla ice cream, softened
1 (7.25 oz.) bottle chocolate shell topping

Drain cherries. Remove stems and save them to complete the recipe. Place cherries and 1 cup ice cream in electric blender. Pulse to combine.

Combine cherry mixture with remaining 1 cup of ice cream in a medium bowl; mix with a spoon. Divide between 2 small (8 ounce) bowls. Cover and freeze overnight or until firm.

Line a baking sheet with wax paper. Shake chocolate shell topping 30 seconds; divide between 2 custard cups or small bowls. Remove 1 container of ice cream from freezer.

Using a small ice cream scoop, scoop 1 (1½ inch) ball; place on fork. Spoon chocolate shell topping over the ball while holding it over the custard cup. Place on baking sheet; quickly insert 1 reserved cherry stem in top. To remove ball from fork, push off gently at base with a knife. Repeat with remaining ice cream. Work quickly so ice cream does not get too soft. Place cherry bombs in the freezer.

Repeat with remaining bowl of ice cream. Freeze until ready to serve. Makes 16 1½ inch cherry bombs.

Tip: If a blender is not available, finely chop cherries and stir into ice cream.

Recipe courtesy of Cherry Marketing Institute

Photo courtesy of Cherry Marketing Institute

There is admittedly a sensousness about maraschino cherries, especially with ice cream!

Engagement

Judith Kerman

82

Even as we are walking through town
hand in hand
and I feel the callus
along the edge of your palm,
ridged like a nail file,
I imagine that roughness
catching on my nylons as you
roll them off, such gentle
invitations, but I laugh and say,
"Don't run them – it's my last pair!"
We stop at the ice cream parlor,
share a cone on the sunny
sidewalk, our tongues
bumping into each other,
the cherry vanilla
dripping all over.

Maraschinos have gotten a bad rap due to urban legends, misunderstandings, and the fact that they contain no actual nutritional value. But they are beautiful, and they symbolize what's fun and bright and sexy in the world. They may not be good for us, although there's currently a "greening" of the maraschino industry. Processors are using a blend of radish and carrot juice for coloring, and flavoring them with natural almond oil and lemon juice. They contain no sulfites or processed corn syrup. But no matter what the process, people love them just the same. They seem to be the perfect embodiment of Cherry-ness.

Poet Anita Skeen explores some of the many resonances of Cherry.

Excerpts from "The Poetics of Cherry"

Cherry, for me, will forever mean childhood. No matter how tempting the royal purple of grape or the sunny disposition of lemon, the sassy talk-back of lime or the trick-or-treat tartness of orange, it was the sweet cherry I went for. And red is not my favorite color. It may be my least favorite color, but when it come to flavors, red is a different story altogether. Here's what I remember about cherry:

Every three or four years, my cousins from California came to West Virginia for a visit. They were surfer boys, thin and tanned and golden haired. One was two years older, one was three years younger. I wanted to be the girlfriend of the older and the sidekick of the younger, a terrible dilemma during my teenage years. But earlier, when we were all pals who roamed the woods and hills in blue jeans and t-shirts, one of the high points of their visit was the making of homemade ice cream. We had a wooden freezer that was cranked by hand, and as my father continually packed the bucket in ice and salt, the cousins took our turn at the crank, churning, churning, churning, until the motor stopped. Then my father pulled out the dasher and we all got a drippy lick, and he packed the ice cream back in the freezer with more ice and salt, then covered it with newspapers and blankets. It was a live presence on the back stoop, groaning occasionally as the ice shifted, the paper floating off to the side as though a breath from the frozen lump had suddenly come forth. My mother made the ice cream, with much debate over what flavor. The cousins favored chocolate, my mother and my aunt fresh peach. My father opted for pineapple sherbet, or vanilla. My uncle didn't care. But I wanted cherry, black cherry or cherry vanilla, with walnuts. I loved the sweet maraschino cherries my mother kept in the refrigerator for topping ice cream sundaes, for putting in pineapple upside down cakes, for, sometimes, dropping smack in the middle of a Jell-O salad or pear half nesting on a bed of shredded cheese. There might be a bowl of white, sweet Queen Anne cherries on special occasion, like Thanksgiving, or the dark red Bing cherries, canned of course. When the neighborhood riffraff broke into our parents' food supplies and filled our haversacks with perishables for some voyage to the center of the earth (often the crawlspace under a house going up on a nearby hill), I took the maraschino cherries, the bread and butter pickles, the dark unsweetened baking chocolate. Let someone else bring the peanut butter and potato chips. Sometimes there were candied green cherries, and during fruit cake baking season, it was easy to slip my fingers into the sweet, sticky chunks and pull out a biteful. But the cherries in the cherry vanilla ice cream—cold, sweet, crunchy—were the best of all.

84

Even as a small child, when the Easter Bunny arrived on Easter morning and left me a rainbow colored basket, I couldn't get excited about the candy. I liked the purple and yellow and green stringy grass on which the candy lay, but I never cared much about the candy. Jelly beans got stuck in my teeth, and if they were at all stale, they cracked and were grainy to the taste. Most of the crème eggs tasted to me like they should be cooked longer, and the malted milk ball eggs vaporized when they were popped in my mouth. Yellow marshmallow chickens and pink marshmallow bunnies were the worst. Not only did I not like the idea, even then, of eating chicks and bunnies, but they were sweet, sweet, sweet and gooey to boot. The foil wrapped solid chocolate eggs got my approval, as did most anything solid or hollow chocolate, though I still had qualms about biting the ears and heads of Peter Rabbit. So my mother (or the Easter Bunny) stopped getting me the traditional Easter candy in the traditional basket. Once I got an orange toy school bus filled with chocolate eggs, and another time an Easter tree where chocolate eggs dangled like ornaments. But once I discovered Brach's Chocolate Covered Cherries, that was my candy of choice. The obsessive compulsive part of me liked to look at all the little mounds lined up in neat rows, under which was another row of neat little mounds. Horse turds, my friend Stevie called them, but what did he know? He liked black licorice, which was like eating coal. I loved biting into the chocolate delicately, creating a little window in the wall, and then sucking all the sweet juice out in one slurp. Oh, heavenly! Then I munched my way around the cherry till the chocolate disappeared, and I was left with one perfect shiny cherry sitting on a disk of chocolate. One more bite, and the last and best morsel was gone. Word got out to Santa about my love of chocolate covered cherries. Each Christmas in my stocking, or below the tree, was at least one box of chocolate covered cherries. My Aunt Grace, who also has a sweet tooth, often gave me a box, too, along with the practical slip or new underpants. Even today, in the Christmas box I receive from her in retirement in Florida, there is often a box of Brach's Chocolate Covered Cherries. She is ninety-eight years old and living in her own apartment, cooking her own meals, going shopping every Thursday morning to Wal-Mart with my father. It's the cherries, of course, that have preserved and protected her.

As childhood gave way to the teenage years, my interests, my habits, and my companions changed. My ragamuffin neighborhood gang was replaced by girls who wore A-line skirts and stockings, who carried purses and wore their hair in flips. Gone were the Lone Ranger lunch boxes and thermos bottles of warm milk. Now we walked on our lunch hour to the Sweet Shop for a cheeseburger and fries, to the Blossom Dairy for mashed potatoes and gravy (this was before we knew of cholesterol), and after school we went downtown to Woolworth's where, bathed in the perfume of Planters roasting peanuts that pervaded the store, we climbed the stairs to the mezzanine and spun a red vinyl covered stool our way, then ordered a hot dog with mustard, onions, and slaw and a cherry smash. Not a Coca-cola, not a Pepsi or a Grapette, but a cherry smash. The fizz, the bite, the sweet liquid seemed a just reward for a hard day in Latin class or second year Algebra.

You couldn't get a cherry smash just anywhere. There were cherry cokes, and cherry fizzes, but they were not a cherry smash. Perhaps there was something about the name that made us so crazy about them when at the Noonday dances we found ourselves doing the Monster Mash or wished our bodies to be smashed up against the khaki clad and oxford shirted boys who were upperclassmen. But for me it was the cherry once again, that favorite of flavors

since childhood, the taste that had accompanied me on all my forays into the world of taste buds, the flavor I had never abandoned as first choice.

Now I am a grown-up, I'm told, with grown-up tastes and grown-up ways. I no longer live in West Virginia, land of rhododendron and coal, but in Michigan, land of the Great Lakes and Traverse City, the Cherry Capital of the World. Up the road, outside of Charlevoix, hangs the pie pan for the World's Largest Cherry Pie, a plate the size of a swimming pool. I have discovered in American Spoon Foods more cherry condiments than I could have dreamed of, from cherry butter to cherry salsa, and I've eaten cherry omelets, cherry pancakes, and cherry barbecue sauce on my veggie burgers. I send boxes of dried cherries at Christmas time to friends and relatives all over the country who bake them into chocolate chip cookies and cook them in their oatmeal. I eat a handful every morning as an anti-oxidant and add them to almonds and sunflower seeds in my trail mix. We have planted three cherry trees in our yard along with pear and apple. Their cherries have provided us innumerable tasty pies. Where I work, at Michigan State University, there is a dairy store with myriad flavors of silky local ice cream. Among the best is Michigan black cherry, rich and nearly purple, with cherries the size of my thumbnail. At the University, I teach in the English Department where I write and explore po-etry, among other things. In my introductory poetry writing course, I require all the students to memorize a poem of at least twenty lines. I've memorized scores of poems over the years as I have asked them to do. Is it any wonder that one of my favorites begins with these lines by A. E. Houseman:

> *Loveliest of trees, the cherry now*
> *Is hung with bloom along the bough,...*

Delicious, simply delicious.

Anita Skeen

88

Fresh faces and phases...

Photo of Emily, Cheryl and Eric Kobernik with their cherries, courtesy of North Star Organics.

Like many modern industries, the cherry business is in a constant state of flux and evolution. From processing methods, to orchard equipment innovation, product development, marketing strategies, and improvements in the fruit itself, Northern Michigan's cherry country is a leader. This section showcases some of Northern Michigan's forward thinking cherry industry entrepreneurs.

Balaton Cherries:
talking with Dr. Amy Iezzoni

In 1981, Dr. Amy Iezzoni completed her studies in plant breeding and genetics at the University of Wisconsin in Madison and was hired by Michigan State University to initiate a tart cherry breeding program. The objective of the research group at MSU was to develop a disease and frost resistant variety of tart cherry. Although the Cold War was still on and the Berlin Wall was still in place, she traveled to many countries in Eastern Europe looking for good potential varieties.

In Hungary's villages, where the tart cherry is commonly found in backyard gardens and along sidewalks and roadsides rather than specifically in orchards, Dr. Iezzoni found what she was looking for. The tart cherries known as "Pándy" cherries are propagated and grow along the lanes as part of Hungarian peasant culture. The blossoms each spring are a common sight in the towns, and people can pick fruit from trees as they walk along the street.

90

Dr. Iezzoni and other staff imported the different breeds they work with in cooperation with communist scientists who were doing experimental work at fruit stations in Hungary. The Balaton's predecessor was released as a commercial variety in Communist Hungary in 1970; it now represents at least 30% of Hungary's tart cherry production. The Balaton was introduced to the United States in the mid 1990's after much hard work and development by the researchers at Michigan State University in conjunction with growers. Local growers of the Balaton include the Gregory family at Cherry Bay Orchards, Inc., in Suttons Bay, Michigan, who are known as progressive growers in the region because of their interest in innovation. Their plantings of Balaton cherries began with 10-20 test trees in 1991, and now they are one of the region's leaders in Balaton production.

To honor its origin, the Balaton cherry now grown in Northern Michigan is named for Lake Balaton, the largest lake in Hungary. It was originally named "Bunched of Újfehértói" based on the way the fruit grows in bunches and the village of its derivation, but the Balaton name was later chosen because it is easier to pronounce and easier to trademark. Each tree is actually trademarked as intellectual property of Hungary. Royalties are charged for each tree purchased for planting and then split between Michigan State University and fruit research stations in Hungary.

The Balaton is more disease and frost resistant than many other tart cherries, resulting in improved fruit quality. In addition, it is a self-pollinator (homozygous). Heterozygous trees need to be planted in pairs to assure pollination. Essentially, homozygous trees make it easier for growers to produce crops with use of fewer chemicals and less discriminated plantings.

Another advantage of the Balaton is that it is an extremely firm tart cherry. When they ripen, the cherries naturally separate from the stem, and the fruit is then naturally protected by a fully developed abscission layer (a special cell layer at the stem attachment which seals off the fruit). Sweet cherries and other varieties of tarts do not have a similar "packaging" ability, so most tart cherries farmed conventionally are sprayed when it's time for harvest to help them separate.

Each variety of cherry is of course different from all others, but here's an easy way to understand just what a Balaton cherry is. Tart cherries can be classified into two major groupings: morello and amarelle. Amarelle cherries, such as the Montmorency, only have red pigment in the skin of the fruit, while the flesh is clear and appears yellowish. Morello cherries, such as the Balaton, have red pigment in the fruit's skin and all the way through the flesh. They are not a dark red like our traditional varieties of sweet cherries, but a shade of garnet. They have a plum-like flavor as they are lower in acidity and are higher in antioxidants than other tart cherries. These traits make them more appealing and diverse in end-product food processing.

The market is beginning to open for Balaton cherry products in many forms as the industry finds ways to promote this new variety. It's been called the first "fresh market" tart cherry, that is, a tart cherry with the characteristics needed to be sold as fresh fruit. Availability will depend on how much interest consumers show. Because it's a darker cherry but has a tart flavor, there are a lot of possibilities for the variety. Grant money has been awarded for marketing this new variety, and Balatons will soon be seen more frequently in the form of dried cherries, cherry concentrate juice, and in wines.

Dr. Iezzoni continues to work within the program at Michigan State University. Twenty percent of her time is devoted to teaching; the balance is committed to research, focusing on the development of superior disease resistant tart cherry varieties and dwarfing precocious rootstocks for sweet cherries. Other current research areas include the genetic mechanisms controlling cherry leaf spot resistance, self-incompatibility, and other fruit quality traits. She keeps a home part of the year in Leelanau County where she can literally enjoy the fruits of her labor with her winemaker husband, Dr. Charles Edson, who is also a professor of horticulture at MSU.

Nels and Michelle Veliquette, former owners of Country Hermitage Bed & Breakfast in Williamsburg, Michigan, served this dish to their guests.

Cherry Bread Pudding

2 C milk, scalded and cooled
6 C bread cubes made from buttered toast
½ C butter, melted
2 eggs, beaten
½ C sugar
½ C dried cherries (Balatons!)
1 tsp. cinnamon
½ tsp. nutmeg
Hard sauce, whipped cream, or ice cream

Preheat oven to 350°. Mix together milk, butter, eggs, sugar, cinnamon, and nutmeg. Place bread cubes and cherries in a well-buttered 2 quart casserole dish. Pour the liquid mixture over the bread and fruit. Place casserole dish into a larger pan and fill the larger pan with hot water until the water is ½ inch up the sides of the casserole dish. Bake in oven at 350° for 40 to 45 minutes or until a knife inserted in the center comes out clean. Serve warm with your favorite topping. . .hard sauce, whipped cream, or ice cream. Makes 8 servings.

Note: One thing to keep in mind when cooking or baking with Balatons is that the variety itself is naturally sweeter than conventional tarts. So use less sugar!

North Star Organics: talking with the Koberniks

A few years ago, local growers Alan and Cheryl Kobernik needed a place to have their organic tart cherries processed while maintaining ownership of the finished product. It didn't take long for the idea of certification for processing organic cherries to become a reality at Triple D. Orchards, Inc., the company where I work. There were lots of forms to fill out and a tough inspection, but it all came together, working with Food For Thought's Timothy Young and Evan Smith.

I've gotten to know the Koberniks well since they began having their fruit processed at Triple D. Orchards, Inc. Some mornings I'll see Alan's truck loaded with tanks ahead of me, his taillights easing up Indian Hill Road, going to the plant. I overtake him so coffee will be ready on his arrival; the small pot in the office only takes a few minutes to brew. Talking with him and his wife Cheryl, I've learned more of their story.

94

"In 1985 we literally 'bought the farm.' It didn't matter where it was in Northern Michigan. Cherries were the preferred crop but other fruits were acceptable. It had to produce some return, have a habitable dwelling, and be affordable. Through word of mouth we ended up with a 40-acre tart and sweet cherry farm in Benzie County. After twenty years of ownership we have uncovered some of the history of this particular parcel of land: Contrary to most farmsteads in the early 1900's this farm never did expand its boundaries beyond forty acres. What a novelty, or is it an anomaly?

"Our ideas and the prognosis of the industry in 1985 suggested one could generate enough income to sustain a family and a respectable lifestyle with some off-season income, as it appeared it did for the past generations. In hindsight, 1985 represented one of the last years that the cherry industry returned a respectful, responsible return to growers for a decent size crop. After that year grower prices spiraled downward to a historic low of approximately $0.05/pound in 1995 with some recovery in recent years, markedly below parity. The share of the consumers' food dollar that trickled back to the farmer in 1910 was $0.40/pound. In 1997 it was $0.07/pound."

The Koberniks entered the world of agriculture with no formal training or family history of farming. Alan's aunt and uncle still have a tart cherry farm in Honor where he spent many summers as a kid and teen. Cheryl's father was a frustrated German engineer and immigrant farmer who grew large gardens on summer property in Charlevoix County. Alan brought the understanding of machinery, patience, and a strong work ethic to the project, while Cheryl brought her understanding of people, her drive, and impatience. Together they have worked to create a home, lifestyle, and income. Cheryl has gotten deeply involved in local, state, and federal agricultural programs, agencies, and committees to better the situation of all fruit producers.

"Benzie County has witnessed orchards abandoned, developed into residential areas, and some have been leased or purchased by growers who believe volume will save them. The most alarming and greatest loss is the dwindling number of genuine growers, their families, and their agrarian presence in our community. While our focus is on the cherry industry, the same pattern is relevant to most other commodities. There are fewer farmers than full-time prisoners in the United States.

"We worked within the system for fourteen years only to realize hard work, product quality, and personal involvement in the industry returned little. Grower prices began falling in 1986 and even with the proverbial carrot always dangling for 'next year,' 1999 brought the crossroad of decision: this farm pays its way growing fruit or houses."

Whether by a twist of fate or by coincidence, Cheryl attended a grower meeting concerning organics in the spring of 1999 at the MSU Northwest Research Station. Alan heard her enthusiastic report, attended a bio-systems meeting in Marlette in organic practices the next week and, as they say, "The rest was history." June of 1998 (the previous season) was the last year that any organically prohibited chemical input or practice was utilized on their farm.

"Our first disillusionment and resulting paradigm shift was from the land itself. One does not control nature. The most one can hope for is to manage it. The word 'control' has for all practical purposes been stripped from our own vocabulary. However, it continues to be a murmur resonating in our heads; a tenacious urge that is hard to shake which nature may annihilate in an instant. Pre-organic practices elicited control: a park-like appearance, an eradication of insects, diseases, weeds, or anything we deemed not necessary or desired on 'our land.' This perceived control required big guns—synthetic pesticides, herbicides, fungicides, fertilizers, etc. in order to achieve a quality crop. Organically, one can fall easily into a substitution theory; utilizing a conventional model and replacing big guns with BB guns.

"Fortunately, we had the foresight to realize this venture would require expertise from non-conventional sources and mindsets. Joe Scrimger is a soil consultant extraordinaire who took us beyond NPK (the three basic conventional fertilizer inputs) to an understanding of the vast biodiversity of the living soil that sustains our trees. He relentlessly and sometimes patiently has prodded, goaded, and pushed us beyond our comfort level. Doug Murray, a pest consultant by conventional title, has taught us to look. Not for something—but to *look, observe, and watch*. It's so important to spend time in the orchard to observe the trees, their bark, growth habits, leaf size and condition, even the orchard floor. What is growing, what is not? All of nature tells us something. Doug has been our interpreter. What we have learned from both Joe and Doug is how to manage some of the variables but also that nature consists of nothing BUT variables. Every one management practice that is implemented usually results in an invitation for nature to reveal the next ten variables that will require our attention."

The Koberniks' farming practices now include semi-loads of compost (not manure), oils from trees in India, chrysanthemum plant extracts, molasses, compost tea, kaolin clay (usually found in toothpastes and Kaopectate®), diatomaceous earth (swimming pool filter material), a copper/lime concoction, fish emulsions, kelp, naturally occurring fertilizers, and even mowing the orchard at key intervals for timely nitrogen surges. Orchard floor management is taken care of by a layered mulching system dubbed "the lasagna method." In place of herbicides, shredded newspaper and hay/straw are applied under the trees in order to add organic matter to the soil, retain moisture, and allow mechanical harvesters to complete their task when the crops are ready.

While they tap the knowledge and experience of assorted individuals and build a base of experience in the uncharted waters of organic cherry production, organic cherry farmers like the Koberniks are fast approaching the end of available resources. They look to the land grant universities to supply pertinent, applicable, timely, grower-driven research for the organic agricultural community. Unfortunately, dependable funding and commitment for such research are hard to find. To support organic farming, organic products must be desirable to consumers, environmentalists, communities themselves, and our government. In that sense, organic practices then require not just an agricultural commitment to research but also a *cultural* commitment.

Organic farmers are well aware that they have just scratched the surface in learning how to co-exist with nature in a symbiotic relationship. This is especially true where the soil is concerned, because the soil, which is the key to organic food production, is a complex living system and fully understanding it requires more research than farmers can do on their own.

The Koberniks' second disillusionment arrived when they were discouraged from pursuing vertical integration. They hoped to set up subsidiaries and a hierarchy of ownership. However, they are a small farm, and their profit margins would have been limited. In addition, it is virtually unheard of for growers to maintain ownership of their own product, including control of marketing and distribution. Most cherry marketing is done by cooperative organizations, and some individuals in various industry organizations and businesses told the Koberniks that one does not, should not, and can not do this. The success of their pioneering idea would depend on finding the right processor to work with.

They were very fortunate to meet and gain the trust of T. J. Keyes at Triple D. Orchards, Inc.'s processing plant in Empire. By working with him they are able to maintain possession of their product after processing. Triple D. sought and achieved organic certification with the assistance of Evan Smith at Food For Thought, just up the road. Their certification made it possible to accommodate the Koberniks' cherries, which required scheduling for special production of the organic fruit separate from conventional product packed during the tart cherry harvest season. This requirement of the certifying board was successfully met.

Seasons for 2003, 2004, and 2005 all showed increased quantity and quality for the Koberniks' organic tart cherries. Though they are always assessing their farm's future, they are likely to continue to pursue organic farming. One absolute certainty for them is that they will not return to the conventional system of farming.

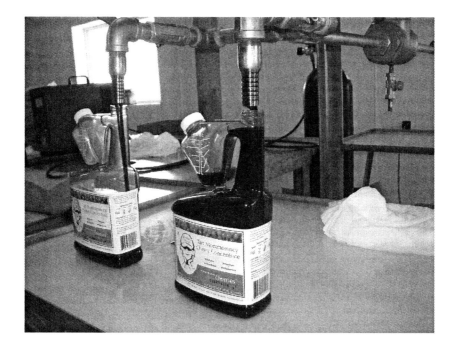

Leland Cherry Company: talking with Michelle White

In 1998 Michelle White was working for a fruit processing company in Leelanau County, Michigan. A divorced mother of young twin boys, she was working full-time and trying to complete her bachelor's degree. Michelle knew that the company where she worked was going through some changes, and she began to wonder about her own job security.

During her time at the fruit-processing plant, Michelle had noticed something she thought might expand her job responsibilities. For years, older people had been coming to the fruit-processing plant and asking for jugs of cherry concentrate, a by-product of pitted tart cherries. All of these people claimed that the Montmorency cherry concentrate significantly relieved the pain and swelling of arthritis.

That gave Michelle an idea: Why not bottle the cherry concentrate and market it to the whole country, letting everyone know about the associated health benefits? As she did more research into the science behind the health benefits of tart cherries, she became more and more passionate about the need to educate the broader public about the many health benefits of Montmorency cherries. Naturally, Michelle was disappointed when her employer made it clear that he wasn't interested in undertaking a national campaign to sell tart cherry concentrate. But Michelle recognized an opportunity when she saw one. So in 2001 she quit her job at the fruit-processing plant. Michelle asked her father to help her write a business plan. Using credit cards to finance the start-up, she went into business for herself as Leland Cherry Company. Sales have doubled every year since then.

Today the company sells not only Michelle's Miracle® tart cherry concentrate, but also Hip Bones™ The Original Cherry Dog Treat, dried Montmorency cherries, and the Cheriskin™ line of skin-care products. They also have started to carry the pill version of tart cherry concentrate, which is more easily consumed by those with digestive sensitivity. The products are sold online through the company's website, and at a growing number of health food and grocery stores throughout the country.

Since starting her company, Michelle has become increasingly concerned about the importance of preserving the cherry farmland of Northern Michigan. In July of 2005, Leland Cherry Company began to donate a portion of every product sale to the Leelanau Conservancy. Founded in 1998, the Conservancy has already protected more than 4000 acres of precious land and 8.5 miles of shoreline to date.

In October of 2005 the FDA warned Leland Cherry Company and 28 other businesses in four states to stop making "unproven claims" about the health benefits of cherries on their websites and product labels. The Agency's letters warned the businesses that failure to correct the violations could result in enforcement action, which could include seizure of products, injunction against the manufacturers and distributors of the products, and criminal sanctions.

They made no suggestions or requirements that marketers couldn't or shouldn't sell these products. And they certainly didn't imply that the products shouldn't be consumed. But the FDA had concluded that some marketers were making claims that the consumption of cherries and certain cherry products could lead to the reduction of symptoms of specific illnesses (arthritis, gout, etc.), and that such claims were, as yet, unproven. While studies by institutions such as Michigan State University and the University of Texas have confirmed that cherries contain antioxidants, consumers should be aware that clinical studies and further research are required before cherries can be considered a "cure" for any ailment.

101

Photo courtesy of Cherry Marketing Institute

Some recipes that John and Michelle contributed use their "Michelle's Miracle" tart cherry concentrate, of course! And of course, one should garnish them with a cherry!

Michelle's Cherry Margarita

1 oz. tequila (Jose Cuervo is recommended)
1 oz. Cointreau
½ oz. Rose's lime juice
¼ oz. cherry concentrate
        (Michelle's Miracle recommended)
Salt
1 lime or orange slice

Shake or blend with ice. Salt the rim of glass, serve with a lime or an orange. Garnish. Makes one drink.

Cherry Chocolate Martini

1 oz. vodka (Kettle One recommended)
1 oz. white crème de cacao
1 oz. dark crème de cacao
¼ oz. cherry concentrate
        (Michelle's Miracle recommended)

Shake together with ice. Strain into martini glass. Garnish. Makes one drink.

Johnnie's Cherry Bomb

1 oz. vodka
½ oz. cherry concentrate (Michelle's Miracle recommended)
6 oz. water or soda
Lemon or lime slice

Mix together over ice, add lemon or lime to garnish.
Makes one drink.

You might want to have the margarita handy for reading Bruce
White's contribution.

Sugar Freeze

Bruce White

Her face and hands: a milk glass setting
on a rich man's table.
They brought to mind bowls of fresh cream
poured over cherries, or perhaps a dish
of ice cream with the cherries already in
it. Sugar Freeze was something young
and virginal, like Eve in the Garden of Eden;
only younger still, with cherries replacing
the apple.
She would lie on her back,
after the fashion of a Rubens in the Louvre,
and confess that she had never had an orgasm,
like saying a real fat snake hadn't been
born yet.

"Life, Liberty, Beaches & Pie": the motto for Cherry Republic

An enjoyable place for people to visit and get to know is the Cherry Republic store in Glen Arbor, Michigan. Its inventive proprietor is a creative hands-on personality who emphasizes fun while creating revenue to support the Leelanau landscape. It is literally Bob Sutherland's mission to place cherries in every household in America. This will help increase cherry sales, keep Northern Michigan farms in operation, and help preserve orchard lands. Cherry Republic donates 1% of their revenue to help the cause. Their plan, started in 2002, is called "*Plus*ONE for Leelanau." It's patterned after a program in Colorado which was started to preserve historic Colorado ranches. They ask retail customers for a voluntary donation of an additional 1% of their purchase to go toward farmland preservation.

This is what the first t-shirt Bob peddled from his car in the 1980's in the Glen Arbor area depicted. He actually sold about 3500 shirts with the graphic designed by his friend Kristin Hurlin. That was the beginning of his "empire's" development.

Bob has created a "destination" in Glen Arbor through his strategic marketing skills. First there was the t-shirt, then cookies, and then more and more cherry products became part of the Cherry Republic. The company offers over 150 cherry and cherry-related products through retail, online, and mail order sales. Cherry Republic takes cherries and adds value to them by creating something they can sell for a profit. Packaging and labeling are key components in product development, but that's just the beginning of their work. They see it as a challenge to create new customers every year while maintaining their old ones. So every day, they need to get people in to sample and purchase their products, then get them to consider purchasing presents from their catalogue, and then get them to actually do it.

The idea of a cherry "republic" seems to fit because upon arrival visitors are immediately welcomed visually by the unique landscaping and gardens, the tantalizing scent of fresh-baked wares, and the whimsicalities placed throughout the grounds. The place is a different state of mind; a republic unto itself. An *Alice in Wonderland*-style Butterfly tree, a teepee, half of a car attached to an exterior-wall, and a chalkboard inside with Bob's pit-spitting achievements are all part of this world at the foothills of the Sleeping Bear Dunes.

Cherry Republic has received a lot of great press: *O, the Oprah Magazine,* placed their cherry soda pop on the "O" list (Oprah's favorite food items). They were listed in *Rand McNally's Road Atlas* as being one of the Best of the Road, and they've been featured on *The Food Network*, in *Midwest Living, Traverse the Magazine*, and other publications.

In a Sunday feature piece from June 13, 1999, *Washington Post* staff writer Craig Stoltz proclaimed Bob Sutherland's empire a must-see for visitors. Stoltz and his family were visiting the area to explore Michigan beaches, but the thing he remembered best about their trip was visiting Cherry Republic. He described it as "Strangely beautiful, delicious and eccentric, rustic and friendly, cool and sweet, rooted in the bounty of the region. . . That strange Cherry Republic store somehow manages to perfectly capture the flavor of Sleeping Bear Dunes National Lakeshore."

106

Everything but the squeal. . .

The Pits

Adrienne Lewis

There was always a cherry
    sitting on top of the frozen vanilla
        with fudge sliding down its sides.

      My father would ask for two,
      but the waitress would come back with one
      bright ruby balanced on a spoon.

At home we had a jar full
      coated in pink syrup.
      The lid always stuck

      and my father would end up cursing
      as he twisted the glass, held it
      between his knees; his face
      as red as their sweetness.

In the summer we stained our fingers
    brilliant with their juices.
      The pits piled nearby

      in the wooden bowl used for salads
      on nights dad would fire up the grill
      and mom set the table.

Say, *they are delicious*
    or *you are delicious*
      and think of them
      before they were picked,

      hard and small,
      thin circles of flesh
      with hearts like stone.

Some of us are familiar with kitchen tools for pitting cherries at home. Usually they're made of stainless steel with hand cranks, resembling some form of torture device.

In the early days of cherry processing, cherries were pitted by workers with handheld goose quills, hairpins, and needles. Then the cherries were packaged for distribution.

The picture below depicts such a scene in a cherry-packing house. An associate of mine who visited a Chinese cherry processing facility in 2004 reports that not much progress had occurred in the processing of cherries there. . . they still used hand pitting.

Photo, c. 1920, courtesy of Benzie Historical Museum, Benzonia, Michigan.

Necessity soon furthered the development of equipment for processors at cherry canneries and packing plants in Michigan. Dunkley International, Inc., of Kalamazoo initiated a line of pitting equipment in 1885 for general agriculture processing purposes. Dunkley's focus was on durable well-designed machines that would save time and maintain the quality of harvested fruit. Each machine has a number of needles that are automated to pierce the fruit cleanly and remove the pit without damage. The processors and growers benefitted by reaping a better price per pound for their pitted cherries.

A pitter specifically for pitting cherries was invented and developed in 1912 by William Decker, then made available to cherry processors in 1917.

For processors, a cherry harvest production season can be greatly affected by the condition and operating ability of their equipment, especially their pitters. Even when the snow is flying, specialists are needed on the job to go over the machines and keep them in good working order, avoiding breakdowns and complications. With proper maintenance, there's a good possibility of keeping machines functional and continuing to benefit from investment of capital long ago. For instance, some Dunkley pitters at Triple D. Orchards, Inc., built in the 1930's and 1940's are still fully operational.

Here's a close look at some Dunkley pitters:

Of course in the grand scheme of things all these industrial details are great. But what about fun? Eating sweet cherries is a fond memory of childhood freedom, especially making that wonderful "phtht" noise when it's time to spit the pit as far and true as possible. There's just something about the woody slickness of the pit in your mouth that makes you feel great as you launch them on their trajectory through open car windows, across the yard, or over a measured line in some form of competition.

At festivals celebrating the beloved fruit, it's customary to have pit-spitting contests. The festival in Eau Claire, Michigan, is focused on the pit-spitting itself. It began in 1974 when Herb Teichman, a cherry grower in southwestern Michigan, was looking for something to do with the pits. His neighborhood competition developed into an international competition recognized by the *Guinness Book of Records*, the Annual International Cherry Pit-Spitting Championship, for kids of all ages. There is a well-defined set of rules for the competition (find them at *www.treemendus-fruit.com*), and the competition even provides denture racks for those wishing to remove their teeth.

The Eau Claire Festival can boast that the first world record for pit-spitting was set by one of their champions—65'2" by Rick "Pellet Gun" Krause in 1980. Rick dominated the sport until his son Brian "Young Gun" Krause set a new North American record of 72'11" at the same venue. Brian topped his own record when he spit a pit 93'6½" at the 2003 contest.

Which is the matrix and which is the gem? It's all a matter of perspective.

garnets

Alisa Gordaneer

i buy a plastic box of garnets
on sale at whole foods
because I can afford this small pleasure,
to imagine myself buying a box
of garnets
to eat.

you don't eat garnets, my small daughter says.
hands me the
pitter. she's learned
i will give her more cherries
if we snap away my fear
into the shape of stones.

this is for your birthday, i say, and mean
this is a gift of cherries, not of garnets
(one standing for the other, though, she
is happy, as long as i eye the way
she is happy, as long as i place each cherry
in the pitter's stirrup, give birth
to a seed instead of the other way round.)

i am mesmerized by red,
as though garnets squeezed from a riverbed.
as though pricked fingers, pipettes of life
months of waiting before she fell
inside me
like a growing stone.

we put the red flesh on our fingertips, fill
centres with chocolate. then all at once
into our mouths: juice, the sweet dark melt,
inventing heaven all over again in a july kitchen.
how you'd never expect.

at last, she insists on eating cherries
by herself, unpitted.
i see stones rolling like marbles
down a long tunnel, looking for somewhere
to stop.
taste the red of my own blood, biting my lip
to let her roll.

At the National Cherry Festival in Traverse City, pit-spitting is a tradition in which even the pageant queen contestants participate. Over the years, it has often happened that one of the candidates won the pit-spitting contest and then went on to become queen.

The many possible uses for the cherry pit stagger the imagination. It was said of the early meat-packing industry that they used "every part of the pig except the squeal," and cherry growers also try to make good use of every bit. Because trees grown from pits are of unpredictable quality, most commercial orchard trees are grown by cloning, taking cuttings of a desirable variety and grafting it onto a vigorous root stock. So it is common for processing facilities to take the bulk of their pits back out to the orchards and plow them under for composting material, returning them to the earth. This diversion of by-product has been common within the industry for decades.

But much more is possible with these woody nuggets. As our natural resources become increasingly strained, pellet and biomass stoves have emerged in the marketplace. It is now common for pitting facilities to sell their pits to individuals who will clean and dry them for use as a heat source. Some businesses carry them in sizable quantities for sale to others. Cherry pits are an excellent thermal conductor, burning longer than corn and retaining heat longer than many natural products.

Because of their heat/cold retention ability, cherry pits can provide great comfort as filling for thermal pillows or cushions. Like barley pillows that have been on the market for years, cherry pit pillows, cushions, and neck wraps may be cooled or warmed for soothing aching joints and muscles. They started to appear in regional shops in the mid 1990's and have been growing in popularity. One of the first brands to come on the market was the Cherry Hug, available in the form of a neck wrap, a teddy bear, or a comfort cushion from Traverse Bay Farms. They can be heated in the microwave or chilled in the freezer, holding their temperature for up to an hour.

Another inventive purpose pits serve is as furniture fill. Manufacturers in Europe have been using them this way for many years. First the pits are sanitized and dried, and then they're crushed to fill the areas of furniture not requiring something plush. This isn't commonly done in the United States, but it's another way to conserve natural resources.

Along the lines of coal in the stocking for naughty ones at Christmas, the folks at Cherry Republic in Glen Arbor offer chocolate covered cherry pits, one more novelty the creative minds of their staff have developed for fun-loving customers.

Once in a while people contact processing plants asking for pits to use as an art material. Mosaics, jewelry, and sculpture have been created by artists and artisans from the proverbial "pig's tail" of the cherry industry. Pits attached to French hooks dangle from ears at festivals and fairs almost every year. In the 1960's pits were fairly common in love bead necklaces, strung tightly together and brightly painted. Googling cherry pit jewelry took me to Beth Kliegerman Tafuri's site, *www.bethsbeauties.com*, out of Mamaroneck, New York where I was able to buy a piece of nostalgia for a reasonable price: a red-stained cherry pit necklace of my very own. Beth had already sold a unique Art Deco handbag decorated with lacquered cherry pits, but she made the photograph available for this book.

Photos courtesy of Beth Kliegerman Tafuri

Dr. Amy Iezzoni, a horticultural specialist at Michigan State University, says she has often been asked why there are no pitless cherries. She explains that although there can be seedless cherries, pitless cherries are not possible.

This is because the cherry is comprised of three tissues—the skin, the fleshy matter we eat, and the pit. All three layers arise from the ovary of the flower. Pollen lands on the stigma of the flower pistil and grows down the style into the ovary. At fertilization a seed is formed inside the cell layers destined to be the stony pit, and fruit development begins. In order for a seedless cherry to occur, the little seed embryo has to grow sufficiently during fertilization to initiate fruit development. After that it is possible for the little seed to abort without stopping fruit development. The cherry looks the same to the human eye, but if you were to crack open the pit, it would be empty.

For a cherry to be pitless, it would have to be without the inner cell layers of the ovarian tissue. However, this is not possible because all three layers of the cherry start out as one tissue. Just as the cherry without the outer layer, or skin, is impossible, so it is with the pit itself. Perhaps further studies in genetics and breeding of the fruit may find a way around this problem.

 Some trivia offered by Dr. Iezzoni: If you see a pit floating on Lake Michigan, it won't have a seed inside. Pits without seeds float. Pits with seeds sink.

At a reading in Ludington in June of 2005, David Sosnowski, an emerging novelist from the Detroit area, read this passage from his novel *Vamped*. This seemed remarkable to me because I got the idea for this present book in Ludington in 2004. To have Dave read this excerpt a year later, when I was in the audience, was pure serendipity.

From *Vamped*:

I'll tell you a story my uncle used to tell.

He and my dad were in the war together—the first "world" one, from before they started numbering them. And they found themselves staying with a family on a farm in France. On their last night there, they get invited to dinner, and dessert is cherry pie. My dad takes one bite and—click!—bites right down on a cherry pit. Here he is, "overseas," having dinner with a nice French family while people all around are dying, and he's sitting there with a cherry pit in his mouth. Not wanting to embarrass his hosts, my dad does what a guy like my dad does: he swallows it. Another bite and—click!—another pit. So, down the hatch it goes. As does the next. And the next.

And then suddenly: "Where are your pits?" their host asks, alarmed.

That's when my dad finally looks up and sees all the plates around him ringed with cherry pits like so many freshly yanked teeth. It's local custom it turns out, to cook cherry pie with the fruit whole, to preserve the flavor.

After hemming, after hawing, my future dad confesses that he's swallowed all his pits.

"In America, they do this?" his host asks.

No, my dad admits, explaining that in America we take the pits out before cooking a cherry pie. He's swallowed his here and now because he thought the cook had made a mistake.

And his hosts splutter with laughter, followed by assurances to my father's reddening face that, no, they're *impressed*, they're *touched*.

They're the old world, patting the new one on its polite naïve little head.

My uncle used to tell the Pit Story while my dad was still alive, to embarrass him, to get his goat, to tease. And he always ended it the same way. "Pretty *pitiful*, eh?"

Except for the last time, that is.

When my uncle told the Pit Story for the last time, it was at my father's funeral, and my uncle left his punch line off. He choked up, instead, his Adam's apple working hard as if he were trying to swallow a cherry pit of his own. Finally, he spit out:

"And that's the kind of guy my brother was," he said. "Kind. He was the *kind* kind of guy. A *gentle* gentleman. It took a lot of swallowing to be that way—pride, mainly, other people's sh . . ."—we were in church; he edited—". . . stuff." He looked up from the podium he'd been staring at. "You know," he said, and we did. Almost everyone around me was working hard at swallowing something. For me, it was tears.

I was just thirteen-dammit and had just started to become the jerk it is our pubescent destiny to become. I was a boy, too, trying to become a man in pre-World War II America, way back when, before people couldn't shut-up about their feelings. So I choked back, and swallowed, and toughed it out, at least long enough to make it to the men's room and the stall next to the wall. Once inside, door bolted tight, I used a big wad of toilet paper to muffle whatever flushing didn't mask.

I didn't think it was possible to hurt that badly again. I was wrong. I started hurting that badly just about every Christmas. My dad died on December 24, just in case I was in danger of forgetting the exact date. So every year I was reminded and every year I resurrected my grief. I missed him. I kept thinking about all the things he was missing by being dead. I wondered what he was like when he was whatever age I'd be turning in the coming year. I wondered what he'd do and what he'd make sure to do *more* of if he knew what I knew about how long he had left.

What would I do in his shoes, with the same number of years?

At fourteen, on the first anniversary, I decided I'd take more baths. Not for hygiene, but to relax. To make my back stop hurting like Atlas all the time. More long hot baths, with a cup of coffee within reach and a slice of cold pepperoni pizza. I'd arrange it so that during these baths there wouldn't be any noise except the sound of the gurgling water rushing out of the faucet. And it could run and run, without going cold or overflowing the tub, for as long as I needed it to. My mother—here was the *real* miracle—*wouldn't* come knocking at the door, asking if I'd drowned, or what was wrong, or did I think she was made of hot water. And when I started thinking about my dad, and all the hot baths he'd never take, that magical tub that never overflowed would know what to do with those tears.

At fifteen, the something I'd do more of also involved locked bathroom doors. Ditto for sixteen. And seventeen.

And when it finally looked like we'd be going to war because of a guy with a moustache just like my dad's, I imagined him giving his hand a rest and signing up. If he knew what I knew about how long he had left—sure, he'd sign up. After all, if he knew *that*, he'd know he'd come through okay. He'd know he'd be around long enough to have a son he could leave too soon. You just had to do the math.

And so I signed up, thinking war was mainly a matter of knowing what to swallow and what to spit out.

David Sosnowski

118

As I hope our book has shown, the cherry is beautiful in all its phases, from the bare winter tree to blossom to fruit. Cherries Forever!

Climbing Cherry Trees

Linda Nemec Foster

Before you can possess them in your hand—
soft globes of perfect color—
you must climb and hang on;
become the tree scraping your knees,
the bark leaving its stigmata on your hands.
Only then will you be able to taste
the color, not just the fruit,
but the color of the fruit.
Deep red fragile skin,
cherry red of succulent heart,
mahogany red of stained pit.
Imagine a stone of pure vermilion
dissolving in your mouth.
The color never leaving your throat
as you sit there in the embrace of the tree
not belonging to the heavens,
but not quite belonging to the earth.

Acknowledgements

I'd like to thank those who made this project possible:

My husband David, for working at the FAA radar "golfball," which led me to sign on at Triple D. Orchards, Inc., for the convenience of the commute; and for always adding to the adventure. And special thanks to T.J. Keyes, my boss, mentor, and friend.

The support offered by Mayapple Press editor/publisher Judy Kerman has been vast and inspiring. Without her, this project wouldn't have gotten off the ground, or off the beach where this idea took shape.

Jim Fredrickson, the crews at TDO, Inc., Jackie Baase & Bill Klein at the Northwest Michigan Horticultural Research Station. Many thanks to the Veliquette family, Norm Wheeler, Warren Deering, Helen Westie, Kathleen Osterhaus—curator of the Benzie Area Historical Museum, *Traverse the Magazine*, Dave & Judy Amon, Ann & Don Gregory, Jose L. & Maricela Martinez, Annette & Jessica Garza, Leonard & Brenda Case, Andrew Case, Jane DePriest, Laura Quackenbush—curator of Leelanau Historical Society & Museum, Amy Hubbell of the Leelanau Enterprise, Rev. Wayne Dziekan, Gladys Munoz, Fr. Rey Garcia, Silvia Cortes, Juan A. Marinez, Cheryl & Alan Kobernik, Dr. Amy Iezzoni, Timothy Young, Evan Smith, Michelle & Bill White, John & Gail Videgar, Bob Sutherland, Michelle Baker, Lynne Teichman Sage, Andy LaPointe, Beth Kliegerman Tafuri, Agnes Fisher of Simon & Schuster, Tim Bloomquist and George Dila.

Thanks also to the many organizations and individuals whose hyperlinks appear on the next page. Without their efforts, this book would have been much less useful and informative.

Information & Resources:

Amon Orchards Farm Market & Bakery
www.amonorchards.com

Beth's Beauties (cherry pit necklaces)
www.bethsbeauties.com

Cherry Marketing Institute   *www.usacherries.com*

Cherry Republic   *www.cherryrepublic.com*

Food For Thought   *www.giftsthatmatter.com*

Glen Arbor Sun   *www.glenarborsun.com*

Indigenous peoples' literature   *www.indians.org*

International Pit-spit Contest   *www.treemendus-fruit.com*

Leelanau Historical Society & Museum
www.leelanauhistory.org

North Star Organics   *www.northstarorganics.com*

Northwest Michigan Horticultural Research Station
www.maes.msu.edu/nwmihort

121

Michigan State University (Balaton cherries project)
www.hrt.msu.edu/Balaton.html

Triple D. Orchards, Inc.
www.tripledorchards.com

Leland Cherry Company   *www.lelandcherry.com*

Traverse Bay Farms (Cherry Hug bears, comfort cushions)
www.traversebayfarms.com

The Cherry Hut   *www.cherryhutproducts.com*

Wikipedia online community-built encyclopedia
www.wikipedia.org

Contributors:

Author **Angela Williams** grew up in Beulah, MI, and was fortunate enough to be able to return to it to call it home. She is office manager at Triple D. Orchards, Inc. Her poetry has appeared in *GSU Review*, *Mississippi Review*, and other journals. This is her first book.

Editor/Publisher **Judith Kerman** founded Mayapple Press in 1979. She is author of 8 collections of poems, mostly recently *Galvanic Response* (March Street Press, 2005). She was a Fulbright Scholar in the Dominican Republic in 2002, and translates Hispano-Caribbean women writers. Her poetry has won the 1999 Abbie M. Copps Poetry Competition, Special Recognition in the 1993 Oxalis Poetry Contest, and honorable mention in the 1978 Great Lakes Colleges Association New Writers Award competition. She founded *Earth's Daughters* magazine in 1971.

Jackie Bartley's poems have appeared in *Image, Gulf Coast, Poet Lore* and other journals. Her most recent chapbook, *Women Fresh from Water*, was published by Finishing Line Press in 2005.

Barbara Crooker recently won the W.B. Yeats Society of N.Y. Prize (Grace Shulman, judge), the Grayson Books Chapbook Competition (Sue Ellen Thompson, judge), and the Word Press First Book Award for *Radiance*. She lives and writes in rural Pennsylvania, where she and her husband are trying to keep a 27-year-old Montmorency cherry tree alive.

Pamela Ditchoff is the author of *Seven Days & Seven Sins* (Shaye Areheart Press, Random House, 2003) and *The Mirror of Monsters and Prodigies* (Coffee House Press, 1995), as well as two teaching texts published by Intereact. Her poems and short stories have appeared in many literary magazines and anthologies. She was a Walter Dakin fellow at the Sewanee Writer's Conference and a John Ciardi Scholar at the Bread Loaf Writer's Conference. She lives in East Lansing, MI, and Liverpool, Nova Scotia.

Linda Nemec Foster is the author of 6 collections of poetry, including *Living in the Fire Nest* (finalist for the 1997 Poets' Prize) and *Amber Necklace from Gdansk* (finalist for the 2003 Ohio Book Award in Poetry). A new book, *Listen to the Landscape*, is forthcoming in 2006. She coordinates the Contemporary Writers Series at Aquinas College in Grand Rapids, MI.

Alisa Gordaneer is an award-winning poet and journalist who lives and writes on an urban homestead in Victoria, BC, Canada. She is editor of *Monday Magazine*, Victoria's alternative newsweekly, and is currently working on a novel, a poetry collection, and a collection of essays. Her previous publications in a variety of periodicals and anthologies include *Three-Ring Circus, Women Who Eat,* and *Breeder* (all from Seal Press).

Conrad Hilberry's most recent books are *The Fingernail of Luck* (Mayapple Press, 2005), *Player Piano* (LSU Press, 1999), *Taking Notes on Nature's Wild Inventions* (Snowy Egret, 1999) and *Sorting the Smoke: New and Selected Poems* (University of Iowa Press, 1990). He has taught for many years at Kalamazoo College.

Rhoda Janzen teaches creative writing at Hope College in Holland, MI. Her poems have appeared in *Yale Review, Gettsyburg Review, Crazyhorse* and others. Her book **Babel's Stair** is forthcoming from Word Press.

Gerry LaFemina's latest collection of poetry is *The Parakeets of Brooklyn*, winner of the 2003 Bordighera Prize and published in a bilingual edition in English and Italian. He teaches at Frostburg State University, where he directs the Frostburg Center for Creative Writing.

Adrienne Lewis is author of two collections of poetry: *Coming Clean* (Mayapple Press, 2003) and *Compared to This* (Finishing

Line Press, 2005). Her work has also been published in numerous print and online literary venues. She currently teaches English at Kirtland Community College in Roscommon, where she is poetry editor of the national literary journal *Controlled Burn.*

Robert McDonough has taught English at Cuyahoga Community College in Ohio for many years. He has published *No Other World* (Cleveland State University Poetry Center) as well as numerous poems in little magazines and anthologies.

Anne-Marie Oomen is author of *Pulling Down the Barn*, a Michigan Notable Book '05, as well as the forthcoming *Uncoded Woman* from Milkweed Editions. She is chair of the Creative Writing Department at Interlochen Arts Academy. She lives in Empire, MI, with her husband David Early and a large cat, Walt Whitman.

Rebecca Emlinger Roberts is a visual artist and writer whose work has been published in *The Georgia Review, The Beloit Poetry Journal, Passages North, Controlled Burn, The Massachusetts Review, The Antioch Review* and others. She has an essay forthcoming in *The Massachusetts Review.* She won the 2006 Abbie M. Copps poetry competition.

Meggan Carney-Ross grew up in Northwest Lower Michigan, which dominates her imagination and writing. She received her MFA in Creative Writing at Western Michigan University. She now lives in Royal Oak, MI, where she teaches writing and is working on a book of creative non-fiction called *Between the Bays* about her Old Mission Peninsula heritage.

Mary Ann Samyn's most recent book is *Purr* (New Issues, 2005). She teaches in the MFA program at West Virginia University and directs the Far Field Retreat for Writers at Oakland University in Michigan.

Anita Skeen is Professor of English at Michigan State University. She is author of 4 volumes of poetry: *Each Hand A Map; Portraits; Outside the Fold, Outside the Frame;* and *The Resurrection of the Animals.* She is Director of two annual creative arts festivals held at Ghost Ranch, Abiquiu, NM.

David Sosnowski grew up in Taylor, MI, a downriver suburb just outside Detroit. He has lived in Fairbanks, AK, and Washington, DC, and worked as a university instructor, gag writer and, most recently, as an environmentalist for the U.S. EPA. His fiction has appeared in numerous literary magazines, including *Passages North, River City* and *Alaska Quarterly Review*. He is the author of two critically praised novels—*Rapture* and *Vamped*.

Evalyn Torrant is a retired teacher working with the elderly. She has had numerous appearences in *The Lyric* and elsewhere. She lives in Midland, MI.

Emily Betz Tyra grew up spending summers on her family's cherry farm near Omena. She lives with her husband Andrew in downtown Traverse City and is the associate editor of *Traverse, Northern Michigan's Magazine*.

Norman Veliquette picked cherries by hand in the 1950's and has spent his adult career processing them. Mr. Veliquette has served as chairman of the Michigan Agricultural Commission, as a district governor for Rotary International, and has published three books on the global campaign to eradicate polio. He grew up and lives near Kewadin, MI.

Bruce White was born in Grand Rapids, MI, but has lived in Kalamazoo for nearly 40 years. "Sugar Freeze" is part of a longer poem called "That's Why They Call Me Johnny Valentine." His poems have appeared in *Gihon River Review, The Offbeat, Pipe Smoker's Ephemeris* and other places.

Other recent titles from Mayapple Press:

Lynn Pattison, *Light That Sounds Like Breaking*, 2006
    Paper, 98 pp, $16 plus s&h
    ISBN 0-932412-40-8
Lorraine Schein, *The Futurist's Mistress*, 2006
    Paper, 44 pp, $13 plus s&h
    ISBN 0-932412-39-4
Rhoda Stamell, *Detroit Stories*, 2006—our first fiction title!
    Paper, 102 pp, $18.50 plus s&h
    ISBN 0-932412-38-6
Douglas M. Smith, Melody Vassoff & Karen Woollams, eds.
In Drought Time: Scenes from Rural and Small Town Life, 2005
    Paper, 110 pp, color illustrations, $24.95 plus s&h
    ISBN 0-932412-37-8
Diane Shipley DeCillis & Mary Jo Firth Gillett, eds.
Mona Poetica: A Poetry Anthology, 2005
    Paper, 114 pp, $16.50 plus s&h
    ISBN 0-932412-36-X
Suzanne Keyworth, *Markers*, 2005
    Paper, 72 pp, $14.95 plus s&h
    ISBN 0-932412-35-1
Lidia Torres, *A Weakness for Boleros*, 2005
    Paper, 48 pp, $12.50 plus s&h
    ISBN 0-932412-34-3
Conrad Hilberry, *The Fingernail of Luck*, 2005
    Paper, 32 pp, $10 plus s&h
    ISBN 0-932412-33-5
Margo Solod, *Some Very Soft Days*, 2005
    Paper, 84 pp, $15.50 plus s&h
    ISBN 0-932412-32-7
John Palen, *Open Communion*, 2005
    Paper, 98 pp, $16 plus s&h
    ISBN 0-932412-31-9

For a complete catalog of Mayapple Press publications, please visit our website at *www.mayapplepress.com*

Books can be ordered direct from our website with secure online payment using PayPal, or by mail (check or money order).

Or order through your local bookseller.